Black Mountains

dinas

Black Mountains

The Recollections
of a South Wales Miner

David Barnes

ISBN: 086243 612 5

Cover: Five flowers for My Father
Mezzotint from Artist Book,
Five flowers for My Father, 1990 by Shirley Jones

Dinas is an imprint of Y Lolfa

Printed and published in Wales
by Y Lolfa Cyf., Talybont, Ceredigion SY24 5AP
e-mail ylolfa@ylolfa.com
website www.ylolfa.com
tel. (01970) 832 304
fax 832 782
isdn 832 813

"…in the sweat of thy face shalt thou eat bread,
till thou return unto the ground;
for out of it wast thou taken;
for dust thou art, and unto dust shalt thou return"

Genesis 3:19

Authorised King James Version of the Holy Bible

Introduction

The peculiar characteristic of the twentieth century was an ever-increasing pace of development, that produced as its only certainty the knowledge that nothing was certain, as its only constant the knowledge that everything must change. Accelerating into the twenty-first century, the phenomenon may prove fatal. We are caught up in storm-force winds of change that give the otherwise inconsequential life of a plain working man from the Welsh Border country wider significance and deeper resonance.

Such a working man was my grandfather. The calm before the storm is set in the hauntingly beautiful, apparently timeless landscape between Monmouth town and the Black Mountains, where, in the setting sun of the long Edwardian summers, a distant past might yet be closely felt. In our conversations together, toward the end of his life, he gave me vivid descriptions of a world we have lost. Of cider-making and hay-making, shepherds and smithies, workhorses and gamboes, hot bread from the oven and cool water from the well, home-cured hams and flitches of bacon, the sound of curlews by day and owls by night.

Although our conversations took place in the late 1960s, what he described was not the romanticised, sanitised countryside then coming into vogue via Laura Ashley. In his childhood, the lanes were muddy, the winters cold and long, and poverty as oppressive as the sultry summer heat. This was a countryside in which my grandfather's two stepbrothers were choked to death by a doctor's fumigation prescription for diphtheria. Where my grandfather, crying with hunger as a farm labourer of twelve years old, gnawed at raw turnips in frosted winter fields and tried to forget the scholarship to Monmouth School he had been unable to take up because his family was too poor. Where the pattern of family life was governed by the seasons of the Hendre, country seat of the Llangattocks, the Rolls family, to whom due deference had to be proffered.

A startling symbol of a new world came out of the Hendre itself. Charles Rolls, aviation pioneer and second son of Lord Llangattock, would not have to fly very far west of his ancestral home, by plane or hot air balloon, to look down on a very different landscape. Here were new Black Mountains: coal-black from those other "flights" that tipped spoil high above mining villages where pithead winding-gear whirred, hooters sounded and slow-moving snakes of coal trucks slithered south to Cardiff, then the world's largest coal exporting port. These mining communities supplied the black gold that powered that new world.

From confinement in the terrible beauty of the Border Country, my grandfather moved to join relatives in the Aber valley behind Caerphilly, starting work as a miner in the Great Universal Colliery in Senghennydd. Within months, at the age of sixteen, he was a survivor of Britain's worst pit explosion, which claimed 439 lives at the early morning change of shift on 14 October 1913. Poverty and Death, the miners called the Powell Dyffryn wagons as they clanked by.

Death, to the point where he was unable to rid his nostrils of its stench, was to be his experience of the Great War. Part dutiful response to Kitchener's appeal, part reaching out again from real hardship to apparent opportunity, the Aber boys presented themselves at the Recruiting Office in Caerphilly and within months were on active service. Their adventure culminated in the Battle of the Somme, that exercise in mass murder devised by a privileged officer class in comfortable conditions well away from the trenches of the Western Front. My grandfather established himself again as a survivor. There is an eerie episode when he found his way into a reinforced machine-gun lookout post on the German line. It had suffered a gas attack and my grandfather looked on in disbelief at a group of high-ranking German officers and their staff cold dead at their posts, as life-like as a waxworks exhibit: a moment of frozen history if ever there was one.

Returning as a miner to the Abertridwr, he raised a family through the locust years of the twenties and thirties, devoting himself to mining safety and building up the local branch of the St John's Ambulance. Practical humanitarianism and comradeship seemed the only valid response to the privations of the time. The comforts of organised religion had lost their credibility. Instead of Sunday school, there were evening classes for the Ambulance and hours of earnest self-improvement by correspondence course, leading to numerous certificates, all subsequently framed for the wall, including a prized first class Colliery Manager's Certificate. But could the cycle of poverty be broken? Poverty prevented all but his eldest daughter, named after the army camp where he had met my grandmother, from taking up the scholarships to grammar school they had earned. All three daughters joined up for the People's War against Fascism, the youngest lying about her age (as her father had done for the Great War) in order to gain admission to the WAAF.

These conversations took place, at a time of unprecedented

affluence, in remembrance of hard times, unbearably vivid for him, almost unimaginable for his grandchildren. Looking back from the vantage-point of the twenty-first century, I realise how ill at ease he was with that prosperity. There was a bewilderment tinged with bitterness felt by men of his generation and background faced with the shallowness of the new consumerism: its easy irresponsibility seemed to deny the values of community life and comradeship in which he had been raised. Youth culture discounted his experience. I have an abiding memory of him with my father bringing me crisps and cider as I waited in summer sunshine outside the Traveller's Rest on Caerphilly Mountain after a morning walk. He took a sip of his first ever pint of keg beer, then slowly and sullenly poured the rest over the ground.

His chronological alienation was compounded by geographical dislocation. He moved out of Wales to Rugeley in Staffordshire following a promotion within the National Coal Board in 1955. On arrival at their new home my grandmother was told by her new neighbour that in England people kept themselves to themselves and were not always in and out of each other's houses. My grandfather sorely missed the fraternity of his own people and spent his declining years at cross purposes with those around him, his attempts to promote discussion seen as argumentativeness, his attempts to organise castigated as "stirring". He was found dead in his garden, where he had been digging a trench for runner beans, on 17 August 1970. We sang 'Cwm Rhondda' at his funeral as he had requested.

What follows is written in the form of a conversation between my grandfather in his retirement years and myself as a young schoolboy already passionate about the past. The detailed checking for historical accuracy owes much to the members of my Monmouth local history evening class for the Department of Lifelong Learning, University of Wales, Cardiff, that first met in 1997, a hundred years after the birth of my grandfather. Their support and enthusiasm over several years proved invaluable in this task of reconstruction. I am most gratefull to Shirley Jones for allowing me to use a mezzotint from her Artist Book *Five Flowers for My Father* on the front cover in exchange for a donation to the St John's Ambulance in Wales. The book is dedicated to my mother on the occasion of her eightieth birthday. Without her, this story would not have been told.

DAVID BARNES

Machynlleth, March 2002

My Earliest Memory

MY EARLIEST MEMORY goes back to the year 1900 when I was just three years old. I had just started going to school in Llangattock Vibon Avel from our cottage, The Garrow, on the Hendre estate outside Monmouth town. You could start school when you were three then, in the 'baby infant' class, provided you had an older brother or sister to look after you. It was a most helpful arrangement for hard-pressed mothers like mine. I had to walk about a mile through the deer-park with my older brothers and sisters and other children from the estate to the main road, which eventually led us to school. We would go down past the big house, over the brook, across the main drive leading back up to the Hendre, then up the hill on the path that ran alongside the thick woods, where the shepherd's hut was situated. At the top of the hill there was a tall iron fence, nine feet high and covered with wire mesh, which protected Lord Llangattock's deer. We had to get over this fence using vertical ladders that had been fixed to either side.

One day, we were making our way to school happily together when one of the older boys – I never found out which one – shouted, "Look out, Alf! There's a badger coming after us!" The others raced ahead and climbed the ladder over the fence, leaving me, the youngest, behind. I screamed and rushed forward, my heart thumping, and scrambled up the fence and over, falling hard to the ground on the other side. Looking up from the ground I saw the laughing faces of the older children mocking me and felt my eyes well up with tears of anger and shame. There had been no badger. I shall never forget that first fright, my earliest real memory. We reached school on time, and no more was said: there was an understanding amongst us that no one ever told on anyone else.

Baron Llangattock of the Hendre

– Tell me about Lord Llangattock and the Hendre.

LORD LLANGATTOCK was born John Allan Rolls in 1837, grandson of the seventh Earl of Northesk who owned a substantial property, The Grange, in Bermondsey, to the south of London, as well a town house in the West End – South Lodge, Kensington – and one in Monmouth itself. In 1892 John Allan Rolls was raised to the peerage as Baron Llangattock of the Hendre, Llangattock Vibon Avel being the name of the nearby parish and the Hendre his country seat outside Monmouth. The Hendre had grown over the generations from farm to shooting box, and became the principal seat of the Rolls family in 1830. Baron Llangattock's father had begun the improvements to the house that his son continued, making the Hendre one of the finest estates in Monmouthshire at the turn of the century.

Georgina, the stern and austere Lady Llangattock, was the daughter of Sir Charles Maclean, leader of the clan Maclean. She cultivated all things Welsh, collecting local memorabilia and bric-a-brac, especially if it was in any way connected with Lord Nelson. She was less interested in her four children. There were three sons from the marriage – John, Henry, and Charles and a daughter –who later became Lady Shelley-Rolls. It eventually fell to Lady Shelley-Rolls to divide the estate following the death of her brothers, each in sad circumstances. Lord Llangattock's eldest son and heir, John Maclean

Rolls, inherited the estate as the second Baron Llangattock when his father died in 1912. He died four years later of bullet wounds received at the Battle of the Somme, an altogether unfitting death for such a shy and sensitive man, who had enjoyed nothing more than playing the organ at the services in Llangattock church. Henry, who was never spoken of, returned to the Hendre from Christ Church, Oxford, after a nervous breakdown, to live out the remainder of his days in seclusion.

The Hendre estate covered over a thousand acres, with beautiful woods, gardens planted out around the house and an extensive deer-park. The deer-park surrounding the Hendre had a very considerable acreage and was totally enclosed by that high iron fence with the wire netting that I leapt over to escape the imagined badger. This fencing was all kept in good repair by the Hendre smithies who worked at the Box Bush forge. The fence was needed because the estate contained over a thousand deer that roamed at will and would come right up to the back garden of our cottage. There were also pheasants, specially bred and reared by the many gamekeepers employed by Lord Llangattock. It was their job to keep a check on poaching of the pheasants and the rabbits that abounded on the estate. My grandfather on my mother's side, John Kidley, was the foreman for the estate, in charge of all the men employed to keep the drives, lakes, footpaths and the rest of the grounds in good order. The gardens were very extensive and were cared for by a separate staff under the overall supervision of the head gardener, Thomas Coomber. Many of these staff, my father amongst them, came into the area from the Rolls family's other properties. I know very little about my father, but he had worked for the Rolls family at The Grange in Bermondsey, then crossed the Atlantic to work for the Du Pont family on their gardens at Longwood House in Wilmington, Delaware, before joining the staff of the Hendre. There was a pineapple house in the walled kitchen garden of the Hendre and an ice house by the yew trees that my father would sometimes take us to see. The large lakes were my grandfather's pride and joy and tending the rare ducks was his personal responsibility.

The high points of the year were the shooting parties arranged by Lord Llangattock and the ice skating parties on the lakes. Everything had to be tidy and well groomed before the arrival of other members of the gentry, and sometimes royalty, at the big house. In October 1900 there was quite a stir when Charles Rolls brought the Duke of York to the Hendre by automobile. At the Christmas house party in 1909, Charles presided over balloon ascents, a hobby he had begun on the banks of the Wye in 1901. I've described our home, The Garrow, as a cottage, but it was a cottage with a difference. It was part cottage, part lodge and refreshment centre. One large room was furnished with oak chairs and a huge oak table. The table had been made by the estate carpenters inside the room using wood from one of the handsome oak trees in the park. In this room and on this table my mother would provide refreshments for the shooting parties, and for this she would earn a little extra to keep her family from want.

Charles Stewart Rolls

– You admired Charles Stewart Rolls, didn't you?

YES, from as early as I can remember, Charles Stewart Rolls was my hero. He was the most celebrated member of the family. He died in an aerobatics display over Bournemouth in 1910 at the age of only 33, the first British victim of an air crash. He had visited Wilbur Wright in Le Mans and acquired a Wright plane, but on that July day over Bournemouth the tail-plane collapsed and he plummeted to the ground.

Crowds attended his funeral in Llangattock church and, just over a year later, on 9 October 1911, at the age of fourteen, I went with Mam to watch the unveiling of Sir William Goscombe John's memorial statue to him in Agincourt Square. He was a brilliant engineer, inventor and designer, who, with his partner Mr Royce, developed the Rolls-Royce engines and luxury cars. He was one of the pioneers of the motor car and of aerial flight by plane and balloon.

While still at Eton in 1892, he wired the Hendre for electricity. Miss Hearne, our teacher at Llangattock School, told us that the Hendre had been the first house in Monmouthshire to have a telephone. That was back in May 1881 when John Allan Rolls installed a Gower Bell loud-speaking telephone in the house. Charles went off to Cambridge where he read Mechanics and Applied Sciences, gaining his BA degree in 1895. At Cambridge he was captain of the university cycle racing team and in the vacations he would ride his tall bicycle along the drives of the Hendre estate to our amazement. To celebrate passing his final examinations, however, he acquired an imported Peugeot, becoming only the fourth owner of a motor car in Great Britain. The following year, the 1896 Locomotives and Highways Act freed motor traffic of some of its restrictions, raising the speed limit to 12 miles per hour. The rest, as they say, is history: he started his own company to manufacture motor cars, going into partnership with a London engineer, Mr F. H. Royce, in 1904, and opening factories in England, first at Crewe, then in Derby.

He enjoyed racing his own cars and in 1906 he broke the London to Monte Carlo record and was asked to write the famous entry on "pleasure motors" for the eleventh edition of the *Encyclopaedia Britannica*. The Hendre had its own gasworks for illumination and its own pumping house for the water supply. With his flair for mechanical engineering, Charles designed most of the machinery for these plants himself and had it made on the estate. He designed and made the mowers and power rollers for the extensive lawns which surrounded the house, including the famous AX 5645 steam roller, and also invented several other ingenious machines for use at the Hendre of which little has been told.

The Garrow

— Tell me about the cottage where you were brought up.

THE GARROW was an out-of-the-way place. To get to the Garrow from Monmouth town you would turn right after crossing the bridge, walk past The Britannia Inn on the Rockfield road and keep going until you reached the Hendre first lodge. Passing through the fine gates and along the drive you eventually came to the Swiss lodge. Here you would pass through the great gate and on up the drive for about a quarter of a mile until you came to the cherry tree. This cherry tree was used by everyone as a landmark. It grew beside a stream that you crossed by walking along a nine-inch wide plank. A footpath through the ferns, which grew tall in the summer, led on up to The Garrow. There was a longer way around the stream for a horse and cart, using a culvert bridge, but most visitors and all the family used the footbridge.

The nearest habitation to The Garrow was about a mile away, a tower built on the highest point of the estate. This tower we called the "look-out", although its real name was the Caxton Tower. It could be seen from as far away as the Chepstow road on the other side of Monmouth. It was occupied by one of the employees of the estate and his family. The rooms were extremely small, yet all the members of this family were very proud of their home in the "look-out", particularly on those special occasions when a flag flew from the pole on top of the tower to show that Lord Llangattock was entertaining important visitors.

My father died before my first birthday in 1898, leaving my mother with four children to look after. I was the youngest, named, so I'm told, after General Alfred Gordon who died in Khartoum in 1885. The eldest was my brother Jack, seven years older than I. He was born in Delaware in 1890 and his middle name was Wilmington as a result. Then came my two sisters Gwen and Nell. My mother had taken her brood to her parents' home on the Hendre estate where her father worked as the foreman. He earned eighteen shillings a week, paid fortnightly, and with this princely sum he supported my grandmother, his two sons who still lived at home, and now his daughter and her four children. Nine of us altogether under the one roof. I remember us all sitting together in front of the fire, as if it was yesterday, the light of the fire on the blue-washed walls. Looking back on that time, I really do not know how he managed, but manage he did. There was never a cross word with him. He loved nature and the estate as if it all belonged to him personally, and he always seemed to have a copper spare for a deserving cause. We all loved him dearly.

There was no electricity in those days, of course. Wood was the only fuel for the house fires and the baking oven. To light the house in the winter we used candles or oil lamps, the oil carried from Monmouth in a tin can. On our way home from school we would gather wood for Mam for cooking or washing. We did have the luxury of a little coal in the winter when a hundredweight of coal would be brought out from the station yard in Monmouth. The coal cost one shilling altogether, three pence for the man bringing it and nine pence for the coal. We treated it like gold, the ashes being riddled and re-riddled for the cinders, to get the most out of it. Good wood blocks and cinders on top made a lasting fire. All the bread and cakes were baked in the huge wall oven, which held fifteen large cottage loaves and also heated the adjoining boiler. We fetched butter and milk from a farm which lay just beyond the estate fence about three quarters of a mile away, and good beef dripping could be obtained at the big house on certain days of the week. We kept chickens that ran about the park, and our fenced cottage garden provided salad and vegetables in season.

My grandmother earned a little extra income by doing housework on neighbouring farms on certain days of the week. Seasonally, she would serve tea in the pavilion for the summer cricket matches, and provide refreshments on the long oak table in The Garrow for the winter shooting parties. She walked several miles to the pavilion and back to do this service and was paid two shillings for her attendance. My mother was an excellent cook and dressmaker. For both occupations she knew how to make a little go far. She could make do and mend, and was a marvel at making old garments into something different, usually by cutting down or turning inside out. Watching her work I learned how necessity is the mother of invention.

The Shepherd

— But you must have moved from The Garrow. I thought the family home was Well Cottage?

YOU REMEMBER ME mentioning the shepherd's hut in the woods, next to the path to school? It was made of wattle-woven hazel twigs coated with clay then covered with ferns. Inside it was divided in two: one room was for the shepherd, the other for his two dogs. To get to the shepherd you had to get past the dogs; no mean task for a stranger. The

18

shepherd's name was Noah Vaughan and the dogs were named Floss and Fly. They were intelligent dogs and the shepherd loved them. A shepherd's life is a solitary one, but Noah was kept very busy at lambing time due to the prevalence of foxes, badgers and polecats in the woods. At night there was no other sound than the rustling of deer, the scurrying of hares and rabbits, and the hooting and shrieking of owls. Noah used the Welsh names for the birds and the animals: when he heard an owl he would open his eyes wide and say, *"Gŵdihŵ."*

The nearest dwelling to the shepherd's hut was The Garrow, and Noah would often come to visit us, bringing his dogs with him, so that we became very friendly. I would walk with him up to the "look-out" which he called *"Disgwylfa"*. He became so friendly that my mother married him and he became our stepfather. Noah was a widower before he met my mother and Well Cottage in the village of Newcastle had been his family home. His forebears had built the cottage themselves with locally-quarried stone. He had grafted the fruit trees in the orchard as a young man. As soon as he remarried he returned to his original home, giving up the life of a shepherd and taking a job as a blacksmith at the Hendre forge at Box Bush a mile or so walking distance from the cottage. His wages were sixteen shillings a week, paid fortnightly. The head blacksmith was Harry Jones and Noah became one of "Harry Jones' men", a much respected fraternity. The new job freed him for the evenings and weekends: his hours of work were from seven in the morning to five in the afternoon Mondays to Fridays and from seven in the morning to one in the afternoon on Saturdays.

He managed to cultivate a big garden, doing battle with the heavy red clay soil, to provide us with vegetables and salad stuff. We always had a couple of pigs at the cottage and some chickens too. A strict chapel man, a Baptist, he would allow no work on Sunday. "The Good

Lord gave us the seventh day on which to rest," he said. "We should ever praise him for that blessing. If anyone is not tired enough after six days' work then he is lazy and should mend his ways."

The Well

– How did Well Cottage get its name?

WELL COTTAGE was situated in the little village of Newcastle on the Monmouth to Skenfrith road. There were just a few other buildings in the village itself, which really consisted of numerous scattered farms. Next to the cottage was the General Store and Post Office housed in a fine building that was once the National School. These building were at the top of a hill, so from the cottage we had the most glorious views of the hills around Abergavenny to the west with the Black Mountains ranged behind them. On a clear night you could see a red glow in the sky. Mam told me that it was the furnaces in Pontypool and Ebbw Vale, and this fascinated me.

The cottage took its name from a celebrated well of pure drinking water which had served the village and all the farms around from time immemorial. We met everyone as they came by to draw water from the well. The water was carried in buckets. Two buckets would be carried on a shoulder yoke with a hoop placed between the buckets to walk in, to prevent them knocking against your legs. The well was a couple of hundred yards from the cottage along the lane, which became so muddy in wet weather it was almost impassable. The well had never been known to run dry and was treated with great respect. The well had a tidy wicker fence, and was neatly bricked around, with a stone slab over the top, leaving the front part open for the drawing of water. As our

cottage was next to the well my stepfather would keep it clean and free
from moss. He was the unofficial guardian of the well and proud of it.
Living water he called it, *dŵr bywiol*. The overflow from the well made
a small stream of the clearest running water that ran across the bottom
of the garden and which my mother said was a great blessing.

Well Cottage

– Now tell me about your new home.

I THINK I TOLD YOU before that my stepfather's family had built the
cottage themselves from local stone, carrying the stone themselves from
the quarry. It was a small dwelling. The largest room downstairs, about
ten foot by eight, was the living room, a room used for sitting in,
sewing, cooking and dining. Here, we children would do our homework
by the light of tallow candles and a single oil lamp. There were two
small windows that my mother would keep open as often as she could.
The room had a large fireplace at one end and next to it, to one side,
was stacked the wood for the fire. The chimney was large and open and
you could see the sky if you put your head in and looked up. Each
spring our stepfather would sweep the chimney, making a good size
brush from holly branches. He put this in the fireplace, climbed on to
the roof and lowered a rope down the chimney for my mother to tie to
the brush. He would then pull the brush carefully up through the
chimney, while Mam held up an old blanket to stop the soot from
falling all over the room. To the other side of the fireplace, built into
the wall, was the large baking oven. It was circular in shape, about five
feet in diameter and about two feet high, and the round oven walls were
clearly visible outside the house from the garden.

Off the living room was another small room with the stairs for the rooms above. This small room was used as a pantry and store. Along one side was a huge stone slab, used as a salting-stone when the pork and bacon were prepared each November. In the beams of the ceiling were large hooks and racks and from these hung flitches of bacon and hams. The pantry had one small window positioned at the foot of the stairs to provide some light. The stairs ran up to a large landing, which was used as a bedroom by my parents. Beyond that, through a small wooden door, was a separate small bedroom, about ten foot by eight, with a single small window, where all the children slept. There was no ceiling, just a steeply sloping slate roof with protective sacking tacked under it, so you could only stand upright near the middle of the room. We had two beds for the four of us, one for the two boys and one for the two girls, with a wooden partition between. The beds were placed against the wall, so the person sleeping on the inside had to get in first. My stepfather would round us up at the end of the day like lambs, calling out, *"Gwely* time! *Gwely* time!"* with a twinkle in his eye. On feather mattresses and under wool blankets, we felt snug and safe, listening to the hard winter rain hitting the slate roof like dried peas. In the autumn we could feel the roof heave during the fierce gales we used to get in that exposed spot; in the summer we would calculate the distance of a storm by counting between the flashes of lightening and the rolls of thunder.

Outside was a large garden. It was divided up into a kitchen garden close by the back door, for herbs and summer salad, with a sage bush growing close to the door and mint that came up in the spring. Next came my stepfather's vegetable plot with its potatoes and peas, runner beans and rhubarb, the latter forced under a broken bucket; then the fruit bushes, blackcurrants, gooseberries and raspberries; and finally the orchard beyond the stream with its variety of apple, cherry, pear and plum trees. Even the elderflower in the hedge could be made good use of and we were refreshed in the hot summer months by Mam's elderflower champagne.

A lean-to shed against the house served as a wash house. In the wash house was a large open copper in which water was heated by lighting a fire beneath. The hot water was poured, using a large jug, into a wooden bath which, when not in use, hung on a peg inside. There was another shed where my stepfather kept all his gardening tools and where he stored his cider. The *tŷ bach* was right at the bottom of the garden, over the stream, through the orchard, down next to the pig sty and chicken cots. We tried to avoid night journeys to the *tŷ bach* if we could.

Telling all this to young people today, they may think we had a hard life, but most of my memories of early childhood are fond ones. As the saying goes, "Be it ever so humble, there's no place like home." I can remember Mam watching the blackbirds nesting in the orchard in the spring and telling me, "Look carefully at how the birds build their nests, Alf, piece by piece, with wonderful skill, and singing praise as they work. That's how homes are made."

Play

– *Did you get on well with your brothers and sisters?*

WE WERE ALL VERY HAPPY TOGETHER and always stayed close, I especially with my sister Nell, who was nearest to me in age. And all the countryside around was our playground. The wide-open spaces gave ample scope for fun and games and we were lucky to be able roam freely in the grounds of the Hendre where my grandfather was foreman.

The staff knew we were his grandchildren and treated us kindly.

In the long summer holidays we would make bows and arrows or slings for hunting rabbits. Or we would cut branches to make quarterstaffs to fight with. We would chase squirrels up and down trees, or make our own hideouts up in the branches and play hide-and-seek. Or look for fancy bird's eggs. When we came across any good feathers we would save them carefully to take to the milliner's shop in Monmouth on Saturdays where we would be given a few pence for the best ones. Here we would pick up boxes from the grocer's shop, tea chests and the like, to carry back home to turn into carts or prams, swings or rocking horses, wheelbarrows or toboggans.

In the autumn we would look under the chestnut trees for conkers. We'd string the brightest and the best of them at home in the evenings and harden them by soaking them in vinegar, before setting out the next day to challenge a friend to a conker fight. In November the farmers or pig keepers would let us have a pig's bladder, which made the best footballs, much better than the balls of rags we used at other times of the year. At Christmas time we would hunt for rabbits and hares which Mam would turn into delicious pies. When the lakes froze over we could skate and slide, and after good snow we could toboggan down the hill by the shepherd's hut.

In the spring we would help keep the crows off the young lambs and help gather wood the woodmen had left behind after felling. Having bundled up the wood and carried it to a suitable place, our stepfather would arrange for a horse and cart to convey it to Well Cottage. At this time of year my stepfather would make iron hoops for us at the smithy, carrying them home for us to play with on the road. What I enjoyed most was hunting for stags' antlers in season after the great stag fights. We would hear these fights taking place deep in the woods and the cry of the vanquished stag would guide us to our find. Generally these fights were to the death, and then the antlers would be ours. We would always report it to the keeper, who would arrange to bury the victim. The antlers would be used to make handles for walking sticks or knives, or hooks on which to hang our clothes.

Most of the time boys and girls played together, although there were some things they did separately. Girls skipped and played hopscotch or played with rag dolls. They were encouraged to make clothes for their dolls and to wash them on Mondays when the rest of the washing was put out on the line. They learned to cook and bake by being given small vegetables or pieces of dough by my mother or grandmother.

The Fumigation

– Weren't you all very crowded in that little cottage?

THERE'S MORE TO TELL about that! I've already told you that six of us moved into Well Cottage from The Garrow. But the numbers grew as Mam started her second family. Four more sons and a daughter followed me in the family as stepbrothers and stepsister. For my elder brothers and sister, this meant that as soon as they were old enough they had to go out to work to make more room for those still at home.

In one terrible winter, when there were seven of us children at home sharing the same bedroom, we contracted diphtheria. As soon as the illness struck, Mam sent a message to the doctor in Monmouth. When he arrived, by pony and trap, he gave orders for us children all to be confined in our bedroom and fumigated for two days. Mam sealed up all the crevices on the doctor's instructions, then waited as he lit large sulphur candles and closed and padlocked the latch on the door. We were told that breathing the sulphur fumes would be unpleasant but would get rid of the diphtheria germs once and for all. It was an awful experience. Two of my stepbrothers, the eldest, Herbert, aged five, and the third, Harry, aged only twelve months, died within 48 hours, leaving only the second stepbrother, Archie, alive, along with myself and my brothers and sisters. How only two of us died I will never know.

Mam was heartbroken. Noah too was badly affected but tried to stay calm. He dared not stay away from work because he could not afford to lose pay for time lost. Our two stepbrothers were placed in little coffins on a table on the landing where our parents slept. The curtains were drawn. Each night before the funeral we had to pass right against the open coffins when we went upstairs to bed. We stared at Herbert and Harry shrouded in cotton wool and once I put my hand in to touch them. They were so cold and still. It wasn't death that frightened me, but that coldness and stillness. Mam told us not to talk and to be very quiet, and we obeyed her because we were afraid that if we talked it might wake them up.

The day before each burial friends and neighbours carried the coffin from Newcastle to Llangattock Church. Harry was buried on 18 November 1905 and Herbert three days later. My parents couldn't afford headstones for the graves but every November, whatever the weather, Mam would pay a visit to that tragic spot.

School

– *Tell me more about going to school.*

LLANGATTOCK VIBON AVEL SCHOOL was situated more or less half way between my old home, The Garrow, and my new home, Well Cottage. School was some three miles from The Garrow, one mile of that across the Hendre park and over the nine-foot high deer fence. From Well Cottage it was a mile in the other direction, along lanes that in those days were thick in the winter with nasty white mud, which stuck to your boots. There were many boys and girls who had much further to walk than we did.

Some of the bigger children came to school on pony saddle, leaving the ponies tethered while they attended school, before the ride home at the end of the day. A nosebag of food was carried for the pony, which was generally slung over the pony's back in front of the saddle. These ponies, tethered by the school during the day, were much loved by all of us. Other children were brought to school by pony and trap or on donkey carts, especially on market day in Monmouth when their parents were passing that way. On market day we would run behind the traps or carts, some of us holding on to the vehicle while the rest held on to each other. There could be as many as six to eight children holding on to one cart until one of the regular passengers would shout, "Whip behind, mister!" and the driver would swish his long whip back to get rid of us. Sometimes the lash struck hard, but no one would dream of crying out.

When I first went to school from The Garrow, at the age of three, Mr. William Lewis was the schoolmaster, assisted by his wife Rachel. He was extremely strict but well respected by the older pupils who knew him best. They talked fondly of his nature walks. Soon after I started school and moved to Well Cottage, Mr. Lewis left and Miss Thomas came as school governess. Three female teachers, two of whom resided with her at School House adjoining the school, assisted her. The third, Miss Florrie Hearne, lived with her sister and mother at Llanvolda, in a house on the bridle path mid-way between the church and Box Bush. She was the same age as my mother and they had both attended the old National School together in Newcastle where they had

had to pay a penny a week. That school closed and became a Post Office and General Stores when the new school opened in Llangattock.

Miss Hearne taught the infants class, a class of about 40 youngsters aged between three and five. She was a wonderful person: she never seemed to get flustered or angry, although we must have been a handful, since some of us were little more than babies. She organised the older pupils to help the younger ones and no one ever felt neglected. We used coloured bead frames to learn to count, to add and subtract. We used building blocks of wood to learn different shapes and how to classify them. Boys and girls were taught simple sewing, such as sewing on buttons, with the girls progressing quickly to more complicated tasks as they became more accomplished. We were taught lessons too, especially history. Monmouth was proud of its heroes and Henry V's exploits at Agincourt were lovingly recounted to us. There were special days when Lord Llangattock would come to visit what he chose to call "his" school. But above all, day in day out, Miss Hearne communicated her religious faith to us. Honesty and truthfulness were all important to her. Somehow she also instilled in us the will to succeed: I remember looking at one of those building blocks, the cone-shaped one, and imagining it to be first a dunce's cap, then a church steeple. Even a dunce, if he tried hard enough, might one day manage to climb a steeple, or even build one.

Sewing or Sowing

– What happened after the infants' class?

MY FATHER had been one of the many gardeners at the Hendre and perhaps this was why I particularly enjoyed the gardening lessons at school. We had our first taste of school gardening at the age of five. Boys between five and eight assisted boys of nine to fourteen. The older boys each had their own small plot and had to provide their own seeds to plant in it. We younger ones helped enthusiastically, bringing in surplus seed from home and tending the plots as directed by the older boys, who, in turn, worked under the watchful eye of the School Gardener. The calculation of plots and rows helped with our arithmetic. In season, competitions were held and our proud parents would come to inspect the plots and witness the judging and the prize-giving. Gardening occupied two one-hour periods a week, weather permitting, and we eagerly made up for any lost time in our breaks. There was also a hen house at the school and we would each take our turn at caring for the poultry.

While the boys worked at their plots, the girls would learn knitting, embroidery, dressmaking and cookery. Again our parents would be invited to the school to see the work and attend the prize-giving. They were very respectful of our teachers and taught us to respect them too. Good attendance at school was expected and I cannot remember missing a day, or wanting too, except when we were very sick and even then to be at home on a school day felt very strange. School hours were from nine till four in the summer, with one hour for lunch and two quarter-hour breaks, one in the morning and one in the afternoon. We would bring our own lunch to school in a satchel: bread and jam, dripping, cheese, syrup, beetroot, carrot or butter. Unless we were given plain bread and butter there was no butter in the sandwiches. It was too precious to use up in that way. We would have a bottle of cold tea or, my favourite, fresh water from the well. In the winter months the lunch hour was reduced to half an hour and school closed early at half past three. That was when Mrs Beti Morris the cleaner arrived, or as we called her, Beti One Wing, because she dusted the classroom with the wing of a goose.

Pupils were given until quarter past nine to get to school. The school bell rang out from the belfry and once it had stopped ringing no one was allowed entry. Mothers knew how long it would take for their children to get from home to school and paced themselves accordingly. Sometimes a pupil would play about too long on the way and arrive late. He (very rarely she!) would then have to return home and face his mother's wrath. Sometimes, thinking to avoid this fate, such a pupil would loiter near the school for the whole day and return home with the others, but the crime would eventually come to light when the parents received the attendance record, and then the punishment would be greater. There were very few late arrivals and justice was administered with mercy: in very bad weather the quarter-past-nine bell would sometimes fail to ring until all those who travelled long distances along bad lanes or over muddy fields were safely gathered in. This seems to me, looking back, to be wonderful diplomacy, for the rule had technically not been broken. It was for her many humane actions and concern for our welfare that we grew to love and respect the school governess and her staff.

Church

— Were you church or chapel?

JUST AS Llangattock School seemed to belong to the Rolls family, so did Llangattock Church, and that was where we had to go. The school was not in any village: it was isolated, apart from a few cottages and farms scattered about. It was situated on high ground some four hundred yards above St Cadoc's Church and its neighbouring manor-house where the vicar, the Revd. MacLaverty, lived with his two daughters, both of whom I resented for the condescension they directed at our family. Mam was church and my stepfather chapel: for some reason I never came to feel at home in either, and my experiences with the vicar's daughters put me off church.

Mam was a remarkable dressmaker. With a needle and thread, or with her Jones treadle sewing machine, she could do wonders. People came from near and far to have work done: an old garment turned inside out to look like new, a father's clothes altered to fit his son, or, her favourite, new ladies' party dresses to be made for farmers' daughters or the gentry. The vicar's daughters were always having work done for them and Mam would work late in to the night to finish the work on time. Nell and I would stay up late with her, making her black coffee to keep her alert as she sewed away. Sometimes our stepfather would lose patience and shout down the stairs for her to come up to bed, insisting that he needed his sleep, and that she would never be paid properly for all the work she was doing. And so it proved. The poor people around generally paid promptly, the farmers' daughters paid after a period of time, but we would wait an eternity to receive our due from the vicar's daughters. They were too proud to come to the cottage to fetch the finished articles and we would have to walk to the manor house to take the work to them and return again on a later occasion to obtain payment.

A path ran from the school, through the fields, past the church and on down to Box Bush where it joined the main drive to the Hendre. This path was tended by workmen from the Hendre estate: there was never a weed in sight and the edges of the path were always well trimmed. All the Hendre staff and the villagers used this path to go to church, attending either morning or evening service as suited their occupation and convenience. Lord Llangattock and his family attended services regularly when they were in residence. Usually they would come by carriage but in fine weather they would walk up the bridle path. John Rolls played the organ whenever he was present, accompanying a mixed choir of about thirty men, women, boys and girls and a large congregation in full voice. The men in the choir all wore surplices and cassocks. The church could seat about two hundred and for the evening service at six o'clock it could be difficult to find a seat. We children then used the kneeling pads as cushions and sat in the aisles. The curate, who lived in the vicarage, read the lesson, unless members of Lord Llangattock's family chose to do so, and the vicar delivered the sermon. Both the vicar and the curate kept servants, the vicar having gardeners also. I was a member of the choir and attended choir practice once a week.

At one point another chore came my way: one evening each week I would walk down to the church to operate the bellows to blow the organ for John Rolls to practise. I was in awe of John Rolls but fascinated by the mechanics of the organ and I can still remember the lead weight that went up and down as I pumped. Little did we know, in those peaceful evenings at the organ, that, within the space of a few years, we would both be facing the horrors of battle on the Somme.

Pheasants

– Tell me a little more about the pheasants.

ABOUT 300 YARDS down the bridle path from the school, towards the church, lived the head gamekeeper to Lord Llangattock, Mr. Annett. Under him were a dozen or more gamekeepers who each had their own area of the estate to look after. Since most of the farms around the

Hendre were rented from Lord Llangattock, who possessed the game rights, the gamekeepers had free access over a wide radius to safeguard his lordship's pheasants. The gamekeepers were paid a pound a week, which was good money on the estate, and many had a free cottage and firewood as well. An ordinary labourer on the estate would earn from twelve to sixteen shillings a week without a cottage. What I most remember about the gamekeepers was their uniforms. They were most conspicuous: a long green velvet jacket with shiny brass buttons and matching trousers. Inside the jacket were two huge pockets, each capable of holding several rabbits. Gamekeepers always seemed able to supply a couple of good rabbits or to get someone to take a few to market for them. "Set a thief to catch a thief," Miss Hearne used to say, and I wonder if she didn't have gamekeepers in mind.

Pheasants were hatched and reared in a special field near the school close to where the head gamekeeper lived. Wild pheasants' nests were sought out very carefully by everyone, including the children, and when a nest was found it was reported to the gamekeeper responsible for that area, who was authorised to pay one shilling per nest provided that there was at least one egg in it. The nest had to remain completely undisturbed. After it was reported to the gamekeeper, he would mark the spot carefully so that he could follow the progress of egg laying until the maximum was in the nest, when he would collect the eggs for transfer to the hatchery.

The hatchery was in a field near the school and close to the head gamekeeper's house, a field elaborately laid out for the purpose. Along one side were scores of hatching boxes. Along another side were the wooden coops to house the fowl hens and the pheasant chicks, while another side again was set aside for the preparation of the feed. All the pheasants' eggs were hatched by broody fowl hens that were obtained from farms and cottages for five shillings each. After the hen had hatched and reared the young pheasants anyone could buy back their fowl hen for a shilling, so it was it possible to lend out a hen and make four shillings profit. On return the hen would be ready to lay eggs again.

Food for the young pheasants was carefully prepared. The gamekeepers went around all the farms and cottages and bought up "surplus" eggs at two pence a dozen. These had to be fresh and were taken to the feed preparation part of the field, where they were placed in large water boilers to be hard-boiled. It was the job of the gamekeepers to shell the eggs, chop them up fine using large two-handed knives, and then to mix in meal to a certain consistency. The young pheasants were fed with this mixture three times a day and had their drinking water changed at least once a day. Special precautions had to be taken to protect the flock and a roster of gamekeepers kept watch day and night against foxes, badgers, polecats, stoats and weasels, sparrow-hawks and buzzards, not to mention poachers: all abounded in the vicinity. There were other predators too: at lunch times we schoolchildren would go down to the hatchery, and while some would draw the gamekeeper's attention away, the others would fill their pockets with hard-boiled eggs that were shared out later, to be shelled and enjoyed.

Eventually, when the pheasants were old enough to fend for themselves, they were taken to various scattered woods, coppices and spinnies and released, in preparation for the shooting season. This was a high point in the calendar when the guests would arrive at the Hendre to party by night and shoot by day with their guns and retriever dogs. All the estate labour that could be spared acted as beaters, forming a line and walking forward across the land swishing sticks and beating the bushes until the pheasants started off to fly towards the guns pointed in their direction. Once shot down they were retrieved by the dogs and laid out in pairs, usually consisting of a cock and a hen, to form a brace. The Hendre beaters were augmented by anyone who cared for a day's sport and who welcomed the extra shilling a day that could be so earned. All were provided with cider and sandwiches, the guests eating apart from the beaters, sometimes at special centres like The Garrow. The signals to stop or start beating was given by blasts on huntsman's horns. Sometimes the shoot would last for several consecutive days; sometimes there were breaks to allow for bad weather.

Thinking about it now, it's hard to believe how much care and attention was lavished on those pheasants for a few days' sport for the well-to-do when there was so much hardship amongst the country people. Few of us would ever taste pheasant but would have liked to taste a few of the eggs we were obliged to sell.

Cider

— You've mentioned drinking cider a few times. Was it made locally?

I'VE TOLD YOU ALREADY about the apple and pear trees that grew in the orchard of Well Cottage, which were the pride of the Vaughan family, many grafted personally by my stepfather. The orchard was so important because the apples and pears were used to make cider and perry. Cider was the main drink in those days beside spring water; tea was drunk sparingly. Each year I looked forward to cider-making time: it was a major event at any farm or cottage.

The preparations were elaborate. The apples and pears were picked from late August through September and stored in the fruit store at the end of the garden, the different varieties kept separate. When the time for cider-making approached, the casks, barrels and hogsheads were taken off the racks in the cider house and rolled down the lane to the well overflow stream to be washed out ready for the new season's juices. These containers varied in size from about nine gallons to the largest hogsheads, which held over fifty gallons. They would be washed out thoroughly, over and over again. A large tun-dish was used to pour water through bungholes into the barrels. Then a length of chain was lowered into the barrel, after the outer end had been secured, so that the water would flush around and the chain would scour the inside of the barrel as it was rocked about. Once clean, each container was tested to make sure that there were no leaks. If a barrel was found to leak, the hoops were slackened off slightly, the leak was marked and a length of reed forced into the joint between the staves. The hoops were then tightened again and the barrel tested to see if it was now sound. Great skill was needed to carry out these repairs but I never knew my stepfather to fail. Once clean and sound the barrels were judged sweet, that is, ready to take new cider, and were placed back on their respective racks in the cider house.

Then came cider-making day. Farmers generally had their own cider mills and presses. The cottagers could take their apples to a local farm or, if they had a lot of fruit like us, they could hire a travelling cider mill and press and have the work done at home close to the fruit store and cider house. The mill consisted of a stationary circular trough holding a heavy millstone, pulled around the trough by a horse harnessed to a stout pole. The fruit was placed in the trough in suitable quantities and crushed under the millstone to a pulp. Spring water was added to the pulp as it was being crushed, the right quantity for the desired strength and keeping properties of the cider, an amount known to the cider miller. When the mixture was right, the pulp was placed in thick woollen blankets, the edges folded over to prevent leakage. These filled blankets were lain one on top of the other until about ten deep, the capacity of the press. The bottom of the press was made of very stout wood, flat in the centre but curved up at the sides like a dish. The full blankets were placed on the flat central portion of the base and a heavy wooden lid the same size as the base was lifted on to the top blanket. Great care was taken to ensure that the edges of the blanket did not come free, for then the pulp would come out and the press would not work properly. A large screw was set in the frame of the press and, one at a time, long press poles were inserted into the holes in the screw cap. Men walked round the press pushing the poles so that the huge lid was pressed down by the screw, squeezing the pulp in the blankets until the juice poured out into the dish at the base. There it was collected in buckets before being transferred to barrels in the cider house for fermentation. When the lid had been screwed down as far as it could go and the press was complete, the pulp would be quite dry. The press would be slackened, the blankets taken off one by one and the dry husks of the pulp removed.

The cider mill and press might be in use for several days, starting early in the morning till late at night. The whole event was a source of endless interest and enjoyment for us children and for our parents there was the satisfaction of having prepared good cider and perry for another year. And how good it was! I never tasted its like again.

Kitchens

– Did your mother do all her own baking?

THE HEART OF OUR HOME was the living room where we spent most of our time together, and the focus of the room was the large open fire that was never allowed to go out. Even when the chimney was swept in the spring the embers were covered so that they could be revived once the job was done. Wood was the main fuel and we children were always gathering fresh supplies, often wet, and stacking them next to the fire to dry. It would take two children a good deal of time on a Saturday afternoon to gather sufficient wood for Monday's washing, as the boiler fire had to be kept going all day. Later in the week, once the washing was dry on the clothes-line, the irons had to be heated on the fire so the ironing could be done. Mam did all the washing, ironing, cooking, baking, sewing – for her own family and the work she took in from outside – knitting and mending as well as helping with the poultry and the kitchen garden. Truly, a woman's work was never done.

Special wood was used for baking, which was done once a week in the baking oven. Mam would bake about twenty large loaves of bread each week and after the bread had been taken out she would bake cakes and special treats for the children: you can imagine how much we looked forward to baking day! The dough for the bread was mixed on the kitchen table, then placed in earthenware jars to rest, then kneaded again on the table, and finally placed near the oven to rise in pans while the fire for the oven was lit and the heat increased. My sisters, Nell and Gwen, would help, and even little Elsie would be given some dough to shape and bake. Mam always knew when the oven was ready; the pans would be moved away from the oven, the ashes cleaned out and the oven floor swept with a broom bosum, the broom giving a distinctive flavour to the bread. The dough was then quickly shaped into loaves on the table and placed deep in the hot oven using a long-handled wooden baker's shovel. When the oven was full, the door would be closed gently and the bread left to bake.

Nell and I liked to make toast. We would sit in front of the open fire, each holding a long, wire toasting fork. We would hold the fork with one hand while with the other we fed the fire with twigs to keep a good heat, removing each piece of toast as it was done and making a pile large enough for all eight of us. Mam would take each slice of toast and spread on beef dripping or lard with salt and pepper. The lard was our own, rendered down - another job for my mother - after the pig was killed on St Martin's Day. The beef dripping was obtained from the big house at the Hendre. Once a week, before going to school, most of the children of employees on the estate would call in at the Hendre kitchen to see the cook, each with a basket in one hand and a shilling in the other. A five-mile walk for us, all told, by the time we got to school. It did make us appreciate that beef dripping on toast.

The old cook at the Hendre was a lovely person. She always filled our basket with dripping and always gave us piece of cake to eat as we walked back home. She gave the impression that this cake was a special favour to us alone but we knew that she treated all the children alike. There were times when we didn't have the shilling but the cook never refused us. Our eyes would open wide when we glimpsed inside the big house and saw the servants, butlers, footmen, pageboys, and cooks in their different uniforms: it was a completely different world.

Mam would ask Nell and me to call by at the manor on our way to the Hendre kitchen to fetch the dripping and say that we must have at least a shilling of the debt for her dressmaking to enable us to pay it. We were to say this even if we had been given a shilling, as well as the times when we had not. Many times the proud daughters of the vicar would not even come to the door to see us but would send a servant with threepence or sixpence off the debt. My stepfather was not to know of these difficulties, and why Mam went on doing work for them before the old debts were cleared I could never understand.

Butter

– So butter was something of a luxury?

OF THE SEVERAL MARKETS within reach of Newcastle, the two we most frequented were Monmouth Produce on a Friday and Abergavenny Produce on a Tuesday. At these markets the local farmers' wives sold their fruit, dressed poultry, eggs, cheese and butter. Mam also supplemented her income by having me help with the butter-making at nearby Newcastle Farm.

The evening before market day was a very busy time for the farmer's wife. After school Nell and I would go to the farm dairy to help. We took charge of two essentials: the supply of fresh dock leaves to wrap the butter and of spring water from our well to keep the butter cool and fresh. On our way home from school on Mondays and Thursdays we would pick enough large dock leaves. After tea with Mam at the kitchen table, I would take a basket and a one gallon milk can to the well, wash the dock leaves and lay them flat in the basket, then fill the milk can with spring water and set off to Newcastle Farm.

The farmer's wife would greet us at the dairy and straight away would pour the cool spring water out of the can into large earthenware pans, just enough to cover the bottoms, ready to keep the newly-churned butter fresh. Then we were set to work. My first job was to turn the handle of the milk separator to separate the cream from the skim milk. The skim milk was put to one side for the time being and the cream placed in the churn, a fairly large barrel on a frame with an axle and a handle to rotate it. I would help churn the butter, which took a long time and was hard work. The barrel was turned on its long axis as this shook the cream more and made the butter form more quickly.

The lid of the barrel, which was clamped down, was fitted with a small glass window so we could see the butter being formed, the first sign being butter sticking to the inside of the glass.

While I churned the butter, my sister would help the farmer's wife to clean and pack her eggs and stack the cheeses ready for market. Once the butter was churned, I would be rewarded with a bowl of *cawl*, fresh bread and a slice of cake. It was a joy to rest and eat and marvel at the nimbleness of the farmer's wife as she used her wooden butter pats to make up the butter lots and weigh them: her hands never once touched the butter. Two of my dock leaves would be placed on the scales, then a portion of butter on top, then the leaves and the butter would be picked up together and transferred to the earthenware pans in half pound lots, all using only the butter pats. Butter from Newcastle Farm had its own distinctive shape and pattern: each half-pound portion was round and decorated with a print of a cow standing under an oak tree. There was something very satisfying in seeing the finished butter, bright and golden and ready for market.

I would help wash out the churn and the separator with boiling water and the farmer's wife was always grateful. "You can't go home with an empty basket and an empty milk can," she would say every time, putting a pound or more of newly churned butter into my basket and filling the can with milk. I took these home with pride: here was enough milk for a large creamy rice pudding and enough to spare to make our morning porridge with milk too. The joy in Mam's eyes was the greatest satisfaction of all.

Tarring the Fence

— Not all the jobs you did were as pleasant as making butter, were they?

NO, INDEED! One of the most horrible jobs that ever came my way was a summer job I had as a child on the Hendre estate. My stepfather bargained with the estate agent for the contract to tar the high deer fence that enclosed the park and the work always coincided with my school summer holidays. I acted as his mate and was paid on a piece work rate at two pence per linear yard of tarred fence, the fence first cleaned with a wire brush. This fence had iron uprights about four feet apart fitted with horizontal iron slats set about two feet apart. The fence was nine feet high and had wire mesh along one side from the ground up to four feet in height to stop the deer from breaking through. So you can imagine the work involved in maintaining this fence, which ran around the entire length of the park.

In the fierce heat of summer we would be stripped to our waists, reaching up to coat the fence evenly with the tar, and getting splashed all over. We carried oil with us in a can that we rubbed on our hands and faces to stop the tar from sticking. We also carried bread and cheese and bottles of cold tea and cider for our breaks. It was a seven mile walk to reach the starting point on some mornings and the same distance back at the end of a long day. Between the hot sun and the hot tar I was burned raw. I never complained to my stepfather because I knew how much he needed the extra money; but, of many less than pleasant tasks which were to come my way in later life, the memory of tarring the deer fence at the Hendre is the most hateful.

Fruit-picking

– What about a happier childhood memory?

WE CHILDREN always enjoyed fruit-picking time. Boys and girls from neighbouring cottages would form themselves into parties and approach a farmer with an offer to gather all his fruit for him. We all knew each kind of fruit as well as the farmer did himself and could distinguish between the different kinds of cider apples and perry pears, preserving apples and preserving pears. We had a good eye to examine a few trees or a whole orchard and estimate the amount of fruit and the problems involved in harvesting it.

This work was paid for at a standard rate by all the farms in the district, namely, one penny per bushel for cider or perry fruit and two pence per bushel for preserving fruit. The cider apples and perry pears had to be shaken off the trees using a long pole with a hook at its end. The fruit would be gathered up into buckets amongst the fallen leaves and twigs, and the buckets emptied into the bushel baskets for measurement before being dumped on to the stockpile. The farmer would pay us by the bushel for this fruit and I never recall us cheating on the amounts or a farmer doubting our word. The preserving fruit, by contrast, had to be hand picked from the trees. The older boys did this, using a ladder and a hook to pull the branches towards them. The apples and pears were picked carefully and placed in a bag slung around their necks. Any bruised fruit was discarded as useless. When their bags were full, each fruit was placed separately in the shallow fruit boxes which belonged to the farmers' wives. The farmer's wife paid for this fruit. All the money earned would be shared equally by the members of the party, and when we returned to Well Cottage we would hand our earnings over to Mam. She would always put aside the fruit-picking money to buy us new clothes and boots for the new school year.

From up a ladder in one of those orchards I could view the whole of my world. I might catch a glimpse of Well Cottage, a wisp of pale wood smoke rising from the chimney and the distant mountains beyond. All around were the rolling fields and hedges I already loved although I knew no other landscape with which to make comparison. The unfolding seasons, the constancy of family and friends, laughter and friendship in the face of any hardship or adversity, and the perfect peace of summer's eve or winter's dawn. It was a peace I would carry inside me, but in my lifetime it was the peace before the storm.

Delivery Boy

— Were there any other jobs you had as a boy?

WHEN I WAS TEN, I came by a part-time job with the local butcher, Mr John Price. My elder sister, Gwen, worked for him full-time and that is how I got the position. Mr Price was a local farmer who killed and dressed his own livestock on his barn floor and then carried his meat around the district by cart, making regular stops for local people to buy what they needed. For those customers who lived off his regular route, Mr Price employed a boy to make personal deliveries to their isolated cottages on Tuesday and Saturday evenings, and at the age of ten, thanks to Gwen, I became Mr Price's delivery boy.

Mr Price's farm, Great Crwys, was about a mile from Well Cottage and I would go there after school on Tuesdays to pick up the bags of meat for delivery. There were several calls to make, up to five or six for each evening round, the farthest cottages up to two miles away, but at least the bags became less heavy as the evening progressed. Meeting the customers was fun: they were pleased to see me and, as time went by, befriended me, so I could look forward to glasses of milk, pieces of cake, biscuits and even some squares of chocolate. There was usually enough for me to take some home with me. Back at Mr Price's farm, at the end of my delivery round, there would be more food and drink awaiting me, together with a large joint of meat to take home to Mam. This was the real perk, for that joint would last us through to Saturday when I would go out on my delivery round again. Looking back I realise what a help this meat was in keeping us all well fed, and wondered whether it wasn't Mam's influence with Mrs Mary Price, whose dressmaking she did, as much as Gwen's, that secured that job for me.

Except for the summer months the walk home from Mr Price's farm to Well Cottage was in the dark. On a clear moonlit night this was fine, beautiful indeed, but on cloudy nights or in bad weather my return journey was in pitch-black darkness. Of course I knew my way across the fields but I would worry that wild animals might smell the meat in my bag: large owls would hoot and fly close by me. I would follow the footpath that went past the ruined cottage adjoining the old Roman road, as we supposed it, that linked the churches of Llanfaenor and Llangattock. That cottage, so they said, had last been lived in by a mysterious character known as Old Jaco. For most of the journey home on such dark nights I would sing or play my mouth organ, to keep myself company and to ward off any dangers which might be lurking. And when passing Old Jaco's cottage, I would quicken my pace, my heart would race, and I would break out in a sweat.

At age eleven I also began to help out at Arthur Rooke's shop in Newcastle, just along from Well Cottage. This was a General Store in the full sense of the word; we could find nearly everything we needed there: clothes, boots, groceries, bacon, bread, cake, corn meal, paraffin and, of course, sweets. For a halfpenny you could buy a "lucky bag" (a bag of sweets with a mystery gift inside), a "knock-out packet" (which contained little models of items of furniture and the like), a yard of liquorice, or what seemed like hundreds of scented "love-me, love-me-nots". Arthur Rooke was keen to extend his business, and so it was that he started to take orders and make deliveries, with me as his helper, working Wednesdays and Fridays to dovetail with my other job with Mr Price.

With an old white pony and a large trap we would set off together up the local lanes. We would go on the cart as far as we could, then I would proceed on foot with a large, heavy grocer's basket to the more isolated dwellings, while Mr Rooke stayed with the cart. The pony was so old and tired it would occasionally stumble, causing some loaves of bread or other items to fall out of the cart and onto the road. Without batting an eyelid Mr Rooke would get the pony and trap back up, pick up the loaves and dust them over, then proceed on his way. Mr Rooke had married the daughter of the previous owner of the shop, Miss Tummey, who taught in Llangattock School. He was always very generous to me, keeping me supplied with peppermints as we went along, and, on condition that his wife never found out, giving me the occasional shilling for my labours. It was not unusual for us to return to the shop at eleven o'clock at night or even later and we would then have to unload the cart and feed and water the pony. Mrs Rooke would then appear on the scene with a small biscuit for me. I stayed for only a year at this job as I could see no prospects in it for me, only for Mrs Rooke.

Leaving the Nest

– When did you leave school?

CHILDHOOD ENDED for me in 1909 when I reached the age of twelve. This was also the age when my elder brothers and sisters had left home to fend for themselves. Somehow I had hoped it might be different for me. I was top of my class in school and Miss Thomas, the School Governess, had let Mam know that I stood a good chance of passing the scholarship examination for entry to Monmouth School. Monmouth School was an ancient and distinguished school, founded by the Haberdashers, that had produced many notable students in its time. A scholarship to go there would have entitled me to an allowance of four pounds a year and, as the school was over five miles from my home, to the free use of a bicycle. It would also have been a dream come true.

Miss Hearne called on Mam one day after school and I could see that they were talking about me over tea and Welsh cakes. Mam was beaming with pride and pleasure. She valued education highly and when I used to creep quietly upstairs to do my special homework (given to those pupils selected to prepare for the scholarship examination) or to work on my models, she would always cover for me. Geometry and science were my favourite lessons and I had a special flair for illustrating those subjects with handmade models. If I remember correctly, I had started making my models the year that school seemed to be forever closed because of the scarlet fever.

I remember a particularly elaborate model I made showing how the earth revolved around the sun and the moon around the earth. I would take each model to school after I had finished it. When I later paid a visit to my old school on home leave from war service in France, Miss

Thomas showed me how she had kept several of my models to demonstrate to the pupils who had come after me. This made me feel very proud, and I could never thank Miss Thomas enough for her encouragement and for opening my eyes to my own abilities.

But my stepfather was no scholar. He could neither read nor write and, what was worse for me, he thought those skills unnecessary. For him, to be able to work with his hands was all that mattered. Hence, though I admired him for his craftsmanship at the smithy and for his talent in the garden and the orchard, I cannot thank him for any encouragement with my education. I was twelve years old and that, for him, meant that it was time I was out to work: "time to leave the nest," as he put it.

I should have realised what was in store for me. Five years before my stepfather had obtained an exemption certificate for my elder brother John to leave school early, to enable John to go with our cousin Edwin Kidley to Mop Fair, the May hiring fair in Monmouth. This despite the fact that he'd just been reprimanded, and the farmer, Mr Morris, reported, for allowing John to work under age at Llangattock Farm. Nell had left school the previous summer to work with Mr Price at Great Crwys. With my younger step-brothers growing up fast and another addition to the household on the way, I can see now that my stepfather simply couldn't afford to keep me at home any longer.

I think I sensed these things, for instead of enjoying Mop Fair as usual, this year it made me anxious. Monmouth was busy and excited as the many local farm servants were re-engaged or hired anew. They stood in the market-place, each displaying a symbol of their respective trades: the milkmaid holding a pail, the wagoner with a knot of horse's hair in his buttonhole, the shepherd with his crook. John and Edwin were there amid the throng, awaiting their destiny.

Empire Day, 24 May 1909, was a chance to forget my worries. On a gloriously sunny day, the Honourable J. M. Rolls visited the school, along with the Reverend MacLaverty. Having been trained in drill by Sergeant Sartin of the Royal Monmouthshire Engineers Militia, we marched on parade around the schoolyard. We saluted the flag, sang Rudyard Kipling's *Children's Song* with gusto, then, forming a circle round the flag, we sang *God Save the King*, before finally being presented with a banana and a bun each by our distinguished visitors. Miss Thomas had posted up a programme for the day produced on her new typewriter.

It was such a happy day that it haunts me still. For, on that same evening, I hugged my Mam, waved goodbye to my brothers and sisters and, with a pat on the shoulder and a firm handshake from my stepfather to steady me, left my childhood home at Well Cottage to join the Morgan household at The Grange Farm.

The Grange Farm

– What was it like in your new home?

THE GRANGE FARM was a large farm situated to the north of the lane that led from Newcastle to Llangattock School. I received board and lodging there in exchange for my services on the farm, before and after school in term time and the whole time when school was closed. This involved getting up at six each morning – at five in the summer – and helping to milk, feed and clean some dozen cows, returning from school to the same task in the evening. Sometimes, especially on Mondays and Thursdays, the days before the produce markets at Abergavenny and Monmouth, I had to return to the farm from school in my lunch hour to help prepare the butter. There were pigs as well as dairy cattle and they too needed feeding and cleaning out. I prepared feed for the animals by putting turnips, swedes, mangolds and beans through a special slicing machine. Mrs Morgan, the farmer's wife, saw to it that I was never idle.

Mr and Mrs Alfred Morgan had four children, the youngest a babe in arms, as I saw when I presented myself to them that summer evening. I was to work with the horseman, or wagoner, whose name was plain Tom Jones but who was known as "Tommy take your Sunday clothes off" because that was the song he always sang when he was feeling merry. He was a born countryman and knew more about the stock that the farmer himself. They both shared a fondness for drink. Tommy never left the farm, although he'd take off for a few days "on the drink" every now and then after some disagreement, always returning as though nothing untoward had happened.

Evelyn Keen, The Nunnery, pale and frail, who had been at school with me along with her brothers and sister, worked at The Grange Farm as a serving girl. I had been especially fond of her younger brother Reggie, who was deaf. We were not allowed into the main rooms in the farmhouse but instead were allocated a bench and table in a back parlour reserved for the farm servants, where stone steps led to our bedroom. Evelyn slept in the top attic and had to be allowed to use the house stairs to get there. I was only allowed inside the farmhouse once during my year at The Grange Farm, when I was asked to rock the baby to sleep but disgraced myself by first falling asleep myself. Mrs Morgan was very angry and set me to work cleaning the harness brass.

Never before in my life had I been truly hungry. I can remember in the winter lying low in the fields, so the farmer wouldn't see me, eating the raw swedes, with tears streaming down my face, so much did I want to return to Well Cottage. So near and yet so far! Had I gone home, my stepfather would not have believed my story and I would have had to suffer more on my return. Evelyn was my guardian angel. We often used boiling water to scald bran for a sick mare or calf. As Evelyn handed me the large kettle she would give a little wink of her watery blue eye and sure enough, each time, she had dropped a couple of eggs in the water for Tommy and me to eat, once out of the sight of Mrs Morgan. When Evelyn was patting butter, she always kept a little aside for me, and when I was fruit picking I would be sure to conceal some choice pieces to share with her. We looked out for one another, and without ever saying much of consequence, grew fond of each other. When I returned home on leave from the war I learned that Evelyn had died of TB.

In the spring of 1910 I had sat the scholarship examination for Monmouth School and word reached me at The Grange Farm that I had been successful. My spirits soared. Evelyn opened her eyes wide with amazement and admiration. I was allowed home for one evening to ask my parents what they thought I should do but it was a foregone conclusion. Mam pleaded with my stepfather but to no avail. I was now old enough to leave school: how could they afford to keep me at home for three more years, even with the scholarship money, when Noah's wages were only sixteen shillings a week? Miss Thomas asked my stepfather to call at the school to see her but his mind was already made up.

I too was learning to have a mind of my own. If I could not proceed with my education, at least I would earn a living. Never again would I work for board and lodging alone. I told Tommy my plan and within a few days he returned from the Duke of Wellington with news of an opening for a farm hand at Garway over the border in Herefordshire. On the following Sunday I walked to Garway, found the farm and presented myself to the farmer, Mr Roy Porter, who agreed to take me on for three pounds a year plus board and lodging. I then had to inform

Mr Morgan, and, a prospect that gave me the greater anxiety, my parents. I had no need to give any notice to Mr Morgan since I was unwaged. My parents, on the other hand, would be shocked that I was going away over the border and I fully expected a mighty row. But, although Mam was upset - I think she still hoped to find a way to get me to Monmouth School - my stepfather congratulated me on becoming self-supporting. So, at the end of that week, I left The Grange Farm and, instead of turning right to take the road for Monmouth School, turned left to take the Skenfrith road to Garway, there to learn some very different lessons.

The Gorsety

– What was it like at your new farm?

MR AND MRS PORTER were new tenants at The Gorsety, a farm that had been allowed to run down, and which came by its unusual name because it had so much poor land covered in gorse. There were lots of sheep, a few cattle, horses and pigs and, of course, the poultry. The Porters were a young couple with a small daughter. They wanted to make a go of the farm and put a great deal of energy into all aspects of farm life. Mrs Porter took charge of the poultry, feeding the chickens herself, and produced fine butter and cheese for the produce markets in Abergavenny on Tuesdays and in Hereford on Wednesdays. She had an incubator, which she called her "magic chick box", which she let me examine closely: she could see how fascinated I was by mechanical devices and patiently answered all my questions.

Apart from me, the only other employee was Mrs Porter's young niece, who worked as the serving girl. I loved working for the Porters;

they treated me like one of the family. We all ate off the same table and were served the same food. The Porters had a small book collection that they let me use and sometimes they would ask me to read to them in the evenings. I slept in my own bedroom in the farmhouse in a feather bed. They were so kind and trusting in every way that I could never do enough for them.

They were church people and we would all go to church together on Sunday for evensong. Mr Porter would only allow the bare minimum of necessary work to be done on the farm on the Sabbath. After the service I was free to join others of my age in the village, provided that I was back at the farm by ten o'clock at night. I admired Mr Porter because he did his full share of manual work. When he set off to the mart he was happy to leave me in charge of the farm. "Keep your eye on things generally," he would say, "you'll find plenty to do." And of course I always made sure that I did. How could I ever let him or his wife down? They set off to market or to town in a gleaming pony trap, for I always cleaned, blacked and polished the harness and washed and polished the trap. I wanted them to feel proud. And they always brought us a little something back from market, fancy cakes or sweets.

One Spring morning, as soon as the Porters had left for market, I made off to a distant field, out of sight of the house, to work on a secret project. I wanted to see if I could improve some of the farm's marginal land. It took me several weeks to grub up all the gorse and stock up the soil on my experimental plot but, when I had done, it looked fairer than any of the other land around it. Next, I swept the hay barn floor for seeds and sowed them broadcast over my secret plot. I didn't say a word to anyone but kept watch to see if the seed took hold and sure enough it did: the new grass was pushing up thick and strong. Mr Porter, it seemed, had not noticed anything.

One fine evening he said to me, "Alf, shall we go up to the bank field and burn off some the gorse now that it's dry?" We went a different way than usual, missing my plot, and spent a good couple of hours burning gorse to clear the land before Mr Porter called it a day. On our way back Mr Porter stopped dead in his tracks and exclaimed, "Look, Alf! Something strange has happened to part of that field over there. It's greener than the rest." I began to laugh and told him of my secret experiment. I shall never forget the expression on his face when we reached the plot: you would have thought that someone had just given him a new farm. He wouldn't move from the spot, but sat down, telling me to run to the farmhouse and fetch his wife, daughter and niece. Then, before the whole family, I had to describe my experiment in every detail. Not completely sure whether I had done right or not, I was relieved to be hugged by Mrs Price as her husband exclaimed, "What did I tell you! The rough places can be made plain!"

Sinking a Well

– You once told me that you had your first experience of mining at the Gorsety. What did you mean by that?

THERE WAS A SHORTAGE of drinking water at one of the farm cottages on The Gorsety and it was decided to engage a local dowser to locate a fresh supply. It was extraordinary to watch the hazel bend and break in his hand when he reached the spot where the well shaft should be sunk. This was where I came in. Acting as the dowser's mate, I was instructed to build a temporary winch and frame and begin to excavate a well shaft, bringing the rubble to the surface in a large bucket. As the shaft deepened, we braced the sides with boards, brushwood and gorse, digging down until the shaft filled with a good depth of water. When the dowser judged the well to be deep enough we made a mat of gorse and shovelled mortar onto it, allowing this to sink to the bottom and settle.

When we returned to the well the following day it was full to overflowing, which puzzled me but seemed to please the dowser. He had me dig a trench on the downhill side to drain the water away. Then we lowered the large bucket, containing a good size boulder, into the well, filling it, hauling it up and emptying it until the level of water in the well had dropped. Using a water wheel placed at a weir we had constructed on a nearby brook, the dowser set a pump to keep the well drained while we lined the sides with bricks, taking care to leave eyeholes at regular intervals.

After a break of several days, the dowser returned and carefully lowered four lighted candles in a bucket into the well. This, he explained, was to test for gas: if "black damp" were present, the candles would go out. The flames burned normally, however, and the dowser had me lower him to the bottom of the well, then hoist him up slowly so that he could test for gas at each eyehole, before plugging them with mortar.

I had relatives back in Newcastle and Llangattock who had gone to work as miners in the Aber valley near Caerphilly and they had told me stories of gas, "black damp" that can suffocate the unwary miner and "fire damp" that will cause a pit to explode. Looking back, I realise that the well shaft at The Gorsety was my first experience of mining.

The Old Grey Mare

— What other memories do you have of your time at The Gorsety?

MR PORTER used to let me take the sacks of wheat to Skenfrith Mill to
be ground into best white flour. I would take sacks of wheat, sometimes
with oats or beans for the stock, and return with fine flour and semolina
for Mrs Porter made from wheat supplied on the previous visit. I went
by pony and cart, using the small grey mare. She was old and gentle
and Mr Porter let me adopt her.

On Saturdays I had a free evening, and as I gave Mr Porter extra
help when he needed it, he sometimes extended this free time to
include the afternoon also. It meant I could return home to Well
Cottage to see Mam, give her my washing and mending and take a bath
in the wooden tub. At first I had to make the journey home on foot, but
soon I acquired an old fixed-wheel bicycle from a new friend in
Garway. It had decomposing solid tyres wired on to the wheel that
prevented me using any brake. This bicycle was good training for
circus work! One day, seeing me struggling to come to a halt by
jamming my foot on and off the front wheel while the fixed pedals were
spinning round wildly, Mr Porter offered me the use of the old grey
mare for my next visit home. With great pride I visited Well Cottage
by saddle pony the following week. Noah was mending the wicker
fence at the well and lowered the pail for water for the old grey
mare to drink. I could see he was proud of the young man who was
paying the family a visit.

I only once had a problem with the old grey mare. I was returning to
Garway from Skenfrith Mill with a full load of sacks of flour. I had just
reached the smithy where the road goes around the edge of the

common, when the mare, forgetting she had a loaded cart behind her and thinking she had a saddle passenger instead, took the short cut across the common home to the farm. But, although *she* took off across the common, the cart stayed on the road, tipping right over and spilling flour everywhere. The blacksmith saw what had happened but it was too late: the mare had taken fright and was off at a canter pulling the shaft of the cart behind her, leaving me sitting on the sacks of flour in the middle of the road. Before long, the runaway mare had been caught and returned and the blacksmith had repaired the shafts of the cart with new bolts. I was very worried as to how Mr Porter would react but, true to form, he took no notice of any damage to the cart but instead asked after me to make sure I was not injured. That evening I visited the old grey mare in her stable but I couldn't tell from the look in her eye whether she was ashamed or amused.

Hilston Manor

– Yet you moved on to another job?

YES. Following my fifteenth birthday in 1911, with Mop Fair again approaching, I had to decide whether or not to remain at The Gorsety. Mr Porter wanted me to stay, and I was very happy there, but I had decided that I should ask for more money. Instead of the three pounds a year I was being paid, I asked for five. Mr Porter said this was impossible: he was only just getting on his feet with a poor farm and couldn't possibly pay the sum of money I was asking for. I told him, in that case, I couldn't stay but we parted the best of friends and in many ways I was sorry to leave.

Tramping back to Well Cottage, I saw a hive of activity in the grounds of Hilston Manor. This beautiful house, formerly owned by the Needham family, who are buried at St Maughans, stood where an earlier property had been accidentally destroyed by fire in 1838. It was now in the possession of the Graham family, and Mr Douglas Graham, who had inherited the property from his father a few years earlier, had decided to add a new wing to the house.

Boldly, I walked up the drive to investigate. A firm from Tewkesbury had been contracted to do the work and I was soon discussing the rates of pay for general labourers with Mr Fox, the works manager, and offering my services. The impetuosity of youth! I knew precious little of any work other than farm work and my only experience of bricklaying had been peering down the shaft to watch the dowser bricking up the sides of the well. But I was fit, capable, eager and willing to learn and must have been sufficiently convincing for Mr Fox offered me a job as assistant timekeeper at tuppence ha'penny an hour. This job involved collecting each worker's tally – a small brass disk – at the start and finish of his shift and carefully recording the hours worked by each man in a large ledger book.

Work on the site started at seven in the morning and finished at five thirty, with half an hour allowed for lunch at one o'clock. We were to work six days a week until the job was finished and this was expected to take six months. There was a good possibility of overtime and, by my calculations, I stood to earn at least ten pounds in that six months. That was nearly as much as my stepfather was earning at the Hendre forge!

There were different rates of pay for different skills. There were – in ascending order of pay – general labourers, navvies, bricklayers, and stone masons, the latter dressing the stone for the outside walls. The general labourers who stayed at ground level, fetching and carrying the bricks and the stone or mixing mortar, were paid at the same rate as me. Those who ran up the scaffolding with their hods of ten bricks or more were paid a little extra. The navvies who dug the trenches earned more, with higher rates still for the skilled bricklayers, who could earn up to four pence an hour. The stone masons were paid by the cubic yard for the stone they dressed and earned the highest rates of all.

Some thirty men worked on the site, rough men who had been hired at the Mop Fair in Monmouth, but I got on well with them. Although I was kept busy at the start and finish of each day and at lunchtime, there was slack time in-between when I could easily run errands for the men and Mr Fox expected this of me. For me, it was good to see Mr and Mrs Rooke again in the General Store at Newcastle and they, in turn, were pleased by the extra orders for tea and bacon, cheese and bread that my visits entailed. I would even get a fire going sometimes so that the men could toast their cheese or fry eggs on their spades. For these favours the men tipped me generously.

The most interesting part of the work came at the end. Two Italian sculptors arrived to take up lodgings at Newcastle. Their job was to work on large blocks of granite to make the massive front pillars for the house, and on figures to be set on either side of an elaborate water fountain. They worked on the block of granite with mallet and chisel; one false slip and weeks of work would be ruined. They were quiet, infinitely patient men who kept themselves to themselves, craftsmen of the highest order. As their work neared completion they put away their chisels and finished the job by polishing the granite with a special stone and fluid. I considered myself very lucky to be allowed to help them with this part of the work – and to earn overtime too!

On 9 October 1911, I went with Mam into Monmouth town for the unveiling of the memorial to my childhood hero, Charles Rolls, who had been killed in an air crash the previous year. A grief-stricken Lord Llangattock tried to speak to the crowd that filled Agincourt Square as

Sir Goscombe John's fine memorial was unveiled. When the new wing at Hilston Manor was completed later that month, Mr Fox asked me to stay with him. But working for this building contractor would have meant moving from site to site around the country, in the midlands of England mostly, and taking a risk with lodgings and bad weather. I chose to stay in Wales.

Growing Confidence

— Were you now living back in Well Cottage again?

I HAD LODGED AT HOME while working at Hilston, paying my mother extra money for my keep, which she appreciated. After the building work at Hilston was completed, I was able to move on to a similar job at Pen-y-lan Farm within walking distance of Well Cottage. The new owner, Mr Preece, was about to get married and wanted the farmhouse modernised and new farm buildings erected ready for occupation. By an odd coincidence, the contractor for this work was a Mr Porter, related to Mr Porter of The Gorsety, and, not surprisingly therefore, we got on well together. I could see his frustration in the mornings as the bricklayers stood about waiting for the labourers to mix the mortar and suggested to him that a couple of us labourers start an hour earlier so that the mortar would be ready for the bricklayers as soon they arrived. This idea pleased him greatly and I was soon earning a little extra overtime while he saved considerably more by not having to pay bricklayers to be idle. This job lasted through to January of the following year and again I was asked, this time by Mr Porter, to stay with the team of contractors; but the same uncertainties of work and vagaries of lodging and location led me to decline his kind offer.

I arrived back home in Well Cottage but was no longer the child who had left the nest with such trepidation to start work at The Grange Farm less than three years previously. I was growing up fast: I had learned to respect myself as well as others, to take a pride in my work and to set an appropriate value on my labour. I was also growing in confidence and willing to risk seeking employment further afield if I could find a regular job with prospects.

One idea I had been toying with, which fitted this description, was to look for a job on the railway. So not long after finishing at Pen-y-lan, I borrowed a bicycle and set off to Pontypool Road Station, cycling over twenty miles via Monmouth, Raglan and Usk. I had heard of this railway junction where the line from Monmouth joined the line to the Valleys, and where the sidings were full of coal trucks. When I eventually arrived at the station, I made some enquiries and was soon being interviewed by the Stationmaster and the Line Inspector. They asked me some searching questions about my school days and recent work experience, before testing my eyesight and offering me a job. I was delighted. The pay would be ten shillings a week and there was a free uniform to go with it. My thoughts raced: would I drive an express train one day, or be a Stationmaster or a Chief Inspector? But where would I live? The Stationmaster told me that lodgings could be obtained nearby for eight shillings a week, but this would only leave me with two shillings a week of real earnings. That I was not able to countenance, and the dream castle of my life as a railwayman dissolved as quickly in my mind as I had built it.

The Stationmaster gave me a free ticket for the train back to Monmouth and asked me to think it over. I returned home with the bicycle in the guard's van. Watching the countryside disappear behind the train was very exciting but it didn't change my mind. It was nevertheless a day I will always remember vividly, the furthest I had yet been from my village and the first train ride of my life. I remember the exact date: 5 February 1913.

Down the Pit

— So you started work as a collier?

TWO DAYS LATER I was with my Aunt Nell, my mother's sister, and my three young cousins in Abertridwr. Aunt Nell had married my Uncle Ted Stone, a collier, at Rockfield, fourteen years previously. They moved to the Aber valley, north west of Caerphilly, to set up home. This was 40 miles west of Monmouth in the county of Glamorgan and a different world entirely from the cottages and farms of the Hendre estate. You could see coal, smell coal, hear the clanking of coal trucks on the railway or at the pithead: coal was king, and young men were flocking into the South Wales valleys, where work was available for the asking. Instead of cottages standing in their own small plots, there were long terraces: I moved in with my uncle and aunt at 48 High Street, Abertridwr. My uncle worked at Windsor colliery in the village. My cousins were Elsie, aged thirteen, Ethel, aged nine, and Gwen, who was still a baby. (Gwen caught polio when she was only two years old.) Also in this little house were two lodgers, Jim Davies and Tom Wells. Jim Davies was the full-time billiard marker in the club and Tom Wells worked in the Universal pit in Senghennydd at the top end of the valley. It was Tom who had asked for a start for me at Senghennydd.

So, on the day after I arrived in the valley, I was interviewed by the Colliery Manager of Great Universal Collieries. He was very considerate, taking great interest in my education and urging me to carry it forward by attending evening classes to study mining. And he offered me a piecework job on the night shift unloading waste that would pay more than the standard day rate. After procuring some old pit clothes, I started work in Senghennydd on the night shift of 9 February 1913.

From the beginning, there was something uncanny about the Universal pit to me. At first I thought it was just the coal-black darkness and that I would have to get used to it. I had the meagre light of an oil safety lamp, but the shadows it cast scared me. The phosphorescent glow of the rotting wood gave me the creeps. Deep in the pit, at the coalface, I had to work on my own, and the loneliness also got to me. But there was something else that made me uneasy, which I could never properly explain.

I'll always remember descending the shaft for the first time. We crammed into the cage, the gates were closed and fastened, and the man in charge signalled to the winder man to lower the cage. We descended at speed and I clutched the handrail tightly, taking comfort from the other men joking and talking. With a bump we arrived at the bottom of the shaft. There was no such thing as slow starting and stopping in those days: that was to come later with safety regulations.

On arrival at the shaft bottom I found a huge tunnel, illuminated with electric light, with several smaller tunnels running off it. Each led to a particular district named after battles in the Boer War: Ladysmith, Kimberly, Mafeking and Pretoria. It was a long walk up the main tunnel, which was called the Lancaster main level, before work could begin, and the electric light did not extend far beyond the shaft bottom. I followed the swinging oil lamps of the work party, stumbling in my inexperience over railway sleepers, rollers and lumps of loose coal, listening to the harness chains of the ponies rattling in the darkness. Each miner shaded his lamp to prevent the glare dazzling the miner following behind him, using either a piece of specially shaped tin, his cap or his water jack. The party grew smaller and smaller as men paired off to go to their respective places of work. Some men repaired the roadways. Some worked with the massive engines, some with ponies to draw out stock coal from the face to take to the haulage plane and others went back and fore with ponies to exchange full tubs of waste for empty ones. My destination was Mafeking district and my job was to keep filling those empty tubs.

The Night Shift

– What sort of work did you have to do?

WE ALL HAD TO STOP at the lamp station. Here, the fireman tested each man's lamp and gave the instructions for the day. On my first night, I was paired up with another man, my butty, who showed me where I had to work and what I had to do. He took me to my work place then set off to his stall at the coalface, assuring me that he would be back to collect me at the end of the shift. It was now about eleven o'clock at night and I waited in the dark for someone to bring me my first tub of dirt. It was a long, lonely wait in the darkness, made worse by the eerie sounds of snapping roof timbers and of falling rocks. The whole pit seemed to heave and crack. My lamp cast monstrous shadows all about me.

Eventually, the fireman arrived to see me. He could see that I was looking apprehensive and told me not to worry as my butty was working not too far away. He warned me to hang up my lamp carefully so it couldn't be knocked, which would make the flame go out. If that happened I would have to wait for someone to come and find me. He also told me to keep a careful watch on the flame: there was gas in the pit and if the flame burned up brightly that was a sign that "fire damp" was about. Pockets of this methane gas collected in the roof ways and could cause the lamp's flame to burn up so quickly that it would go out. If that happened, I should crawl to my neighbour using the rails as a guide. I could then either work with my neighbour or walk back along the haulage plane amongst the moving traffic to a relighting station where you could have your lamp relit using special apparatus. Walking amongst the moving traffic was dangerous, and the neighbour would probably not appreciate having someone else share his piece work: either way you'd be losing time and money. So the message was to keep your lamp alight if at all possible. He also told me of another gas, carbon monoxide, which the miners called "black damp", which sometimes collected at floor level and could cause a lamp to go out for want of oxygen. Finally, saying that he would have a word with my haulier to help me until I got on my feet, he set off, promising to be back after he had completed his round of inspection.

Seeing it was my first shift underground, the fireman had kindly undertaken to see that I was booked a good average of tubs for my first few shifts so that my piece work wages would come right. We were paid fourpence halfpenny per tub of dirt and ninepence per tub of walling stone. Each tub contained about ten hundredweight. My job was to unload the waste from the tubs the haulier brought me from my butty working in his stall at the coalface. The tubs of walling stone were the more difficult to handle. With these, I had to lift the stones out by hand then work to build a good dry stone wall for the sides of the heading. The tubs of waste were quickly emptied by shovel and the waste packed tightly behind the stone wall so that the pit was well sealed for ventilation purposes. Once I had got used to the work, I averaged four tubs of stone and eight tubs of waste a day to earn about 36 shillings a week.

At six in the morning of the following day my butty and I came back up the shaft in the cage, handed in our lamps at the lamp room and collected our lamp checks. He arranged to meet me there that night for the start of our next shift together. He seemed pleased enough with my progress. I raced back down the valley to have the cooked breakfast that Aunt Nell had prepared, as keen to share my experiences with Tom as he was to ask me questions. Although he had worked on the same shift, I hadn't seen him at all, and he'd managed to beat me home.

Valley Life

— How did you find life in the Aber Valley after moving in from the country?

I HAD WATCHED those glowing skies in the west as a child and seen the coal trucks in the sidings at Pontypool Road Station when I went for that railway interview, so I knew the Valleys were going to be exciting. I wasn't disappointed. I've mentioned that Jim Davies the lodger was a billiard marker, but there was far more to the Workmen's Hall and Institute than just billiards and snooker. There were performances of operettas, brass and silver band concerts, oratorios sung by local choirs and the place was packed out for magic lantern shows. Uncle Ted played the cornet in the silver band and he took me along to rehearsals and encouraged me to take an interest, which I did. For sports, we had rugby and soccer, boxing and tennis, darts and skittles. The Workmen's Hall also had an excellent library. For the use of all these facilities we miners paid about six pence a week. Both villages in the Aber valley had their own Workman's Hall, or Institute, with a similar range of activities in each village. Senghennydd and Abertridwr competed with each other fiercely in all things, especially at the annual Boxing Day eisteddfod. In August 1913 my uncle took me on the train to

Abergavenny with the silver band to compete in the National Eisteddfod.

Religion was more prominent then than now. The Independents had a long history in the area with Noddfa in Senghennydd and Adulam in Abertridwr. The Baptists were strong in the valley, with Salem in Senghennydd and Beulah in Abertridwr. "You're going to Morgan John Rhys's country," Noah had told me. I had been brought up on the Hendre estate to attend church but the parish church was not in the valley but up the mountain at Eglwysilan. As a result, in Abertridwr, I was neither church nor chapel but I soon noticed that in this valley the men with Baptist connections were favoured at the pit.

Up the mountain there was a whole other world: bare-fist fights, whippet racing and long summer walks to collect bilberries for my Aunt Nell, who would bake a wonderful bilberry pie served with fresh cream from the farm. There were pubs galore, and clubs for Sunday drinking. The real social divide was between the chapel folk, who disapproved of the drinking, and the rest of us. I would enjoy a long walk up to the Rose and Crown at Eglwysilan or to the Traveller's Rest on Caerphilly Mountain. A collier's work is thirsty work: I was used to drinking cider but was fast acquiring a taste for Rhymney Valley ale.

The most surprising thing is how we found the time or had the energy to do so much. As lodgers we paid seven shillings and sixpence a week for full board and to have our washing taken care of. On Saturdays, though, no dinner was provided and we went into the village for fish and chips or boiled ham and tongue. And for all the rivalry between the two villages, we shared the challenges of this new life together. There was one general hospital in the Aber valley serving both villages. All miners contributed two pence a week from their wages to fund this hospital. I was soon to learn how important this institution was.

The Explosion

– You are a survivor of the Senghennydd pit disaster, aren't you?

As I'VE TOLD YOU, the Universal pit in Senghennydd always made me
feel uneasy. It may just be because I was so young and having to work
on the night shift. Boys my age in Abertridwr mostly worked in the
Windsor pit, which probably contributed to the sinking feeling I always
had when I set off to Senghennydd in the evenings. It was fine once I
had started working, but I never liked going there.

On the morning of 14 October 1913, Tom Wells and I had returned
to Abertridwr after completing the night shift at Senghennydd. We had
our breakfast around 7 am and began bathing. I was first, had bathed
my top half and was waiting for Tom to do the same when a dreadful
commotion seemed to fill the house. A neighbour from across the street
rushed through our front door, screaming and sobbing. There had been
a terrible explosion at the Universal pit in Senghennydd at the start of
the day shift. Her father, three brothers and a lodger were all on that
shift. As my Aunt Nell tried to calm and comfort her, Tom and I rushed
to put our working clothes back on and returned to Senghennydd. The
streets were full of people running, talking, sobbing, screaming or just
dumbstruck. Before long the mountains were black with men from
neighbouring collieries coming to our aid.

The following two days and nights we spent in vigil at the pithead,
returning home for our meals. There was nothing we could do to help. I
watched the rescue brigades with great admiration. Four hundred and
thirty nine miners lost their lives in one of the most terrible explosions
in the history of mining. Children on their way to school gathered to
stare at the cage that had lowered the day shift down the pit and which

had been shot like a cannon ball by the force of the underground explosion up into the winding gear. I could see some children knew instinctively that their loved ones had perished. My Uncle Joe Green was a timberman at the Universal but had been off work sick, a lucky chance that saved his life. He had come from Herefordshire to work as a horseman on one of the local farms outside Monmouth and had met my Aunt Rose when she was in service in Rockfield House. After their wedding, they had moved to the Aber valley to set up home. Others in our family had followed, all with such high hopes.

I was just sixteen years old and the Senghennydd pit disaster was a terrible shock to me. It could so easily have been Tom and me, our family and close friends entombed down below. For what seemed an age afterwards the streets of Senghennydd and Abertridwr witnessed the continual passing of funeral processions on their way to the public cemetery at Penyrheol. Sometimes it was single coffin being carried, sometimes a whole group of them moving solemnly along the main road. It was well into the following year before the fires were extinguished and the final bodies brought to the surface for identification. Sorrow was tangible: the dead miners left 500 dependent children, some 40 of whom were born after the explosion and never saw their fathers. Mary Saunders, the neighbour who had rushed screaming into our house with the news, killed herself by drinking carbolic acid the following year, when the anniversary of the explosion came round. There had been a previous explosion at the pit on 24 May 1901 when 79 miners were killed but the scale of this explosion was difficult to comprehend. In some ways, the Aber valley never recovered from the blow. The silver band played "Lead Kindly Light" and "Abide with me" over and over again so that those tunes are for me forever associated with the disaster at the Universal pit at Senghennydd. It never re-opened.

Windsor Colliery

– What did you do next?

FOR A COUPLE OF WEEKS all the Universal men were out of work, but
gradually the neighbouring collieries absorbed all the idle labour that
wanted work. Some men resolved never to go down a pit again. My
Uncle Ted was working as a coal cutter at the face at Windsor colliery
in Abertridwr and needed help driving a development heading some
two and a half miles from the main shaft. He was on piecework and
offered to pay me as one of his assistants. I worked with a more
experienced boy, emptying bucketfuls of water into barrels that were
taken away from the face by horse-drawn drams. It was an
exceptionally wet seam, with water constantly pouring in from the roof
through cracks in the strata. As soon as the seam was reasonably clear
of water we would load coal into the trams.

My uncle only allowed us to load clean coal. This we did by
dragging the free coal with our bare hands and lifting it into a metal
box that held some 30 pounds in weight. The box was then dragged
along the seam and lifted onto what we called a tummice that raised
the box to shoulder height and emptied it into the dram. Dragging the
box, we held our oil lamps in our mouths, biting the handle tightly with
our teeth to free both our hands. We used the same technique when
ripping down the roof, using sledge and wedge to gain extra height. It
was incredibly dirty work, especially loading the dram. The coal was
very wet and black liquid ran down my arms all the time. The air in the
pit was very warm, however, so in some ways this made it less
uncomfortable. My pay for this work was one shilling and ten pence
halfpenny per ton, with three shillings a week extra for working in

water. Each dram contained one ton of coal.

Although it might not sound much fun, I was now much happier. I was working closer to home than before and with boys my own age who came from the same village. This meant that I had friends for the evenings and, as I was now on the day shift from 6 am to 3 pm, those evenings were free. Above all, it was good to be working with my uncle, who really cared for me. Sometimes he paid my lodging money for me by topping up my wages, so that after I had paid my aunt I still had all my earnings left over. He would treat me to new boots – our boots wore out quickly in the acid water of the seam. I never forgot his many kindnesses to me.

A Soldier's Life

– How did you end up enlisted in the army?

THERE WAS A CHANCE for holidays in August when the pits were idle. I had a cousin, Charlie Kidley, another collier, who lived in the neighbouring valley at Llanbradach. He was the same age as me, seventeen years old. We had agreed, one summer's evening on Eglwysilan Mountain, to go to Monmouth together by train for the holidays to visit our family. Our Uncle Tom Kidley worked on the Hendre estate and now lived in The Garrow, the house where I was born. Charlie's father, Ted Kidley, Uncle Tom's brother, had been a regular soldier with the King's Own Shropshire Light Infantry. He lived at Dugmore Cottage on the Rockfield road out of Newcastle and that's where Charlie was to stay. I would return to Well Cottage to stay with my mother and stepfather.

That August 1914 all the talk was of war with Germany. Uncle Tom was a volunteer with the 2nd Monmouth Territorials and on the day before we arrived he received his call-up papers for the war. We arrived on the Monday in time to watch him march with his regiment through Monmouth town to board a special train at Troy station. Monmouth was a garrison town, the home of the Monmouth Royal Engineers as well as the Territorials. It was also the home of Henry V of Agincourt fame, so patriotic fervour ran high. The send-off at Troy station was a high-spirited and festive occasion, with much laughing and joking as the men were hugged and bid good-bye. "See you again soon!" and "It won't last long!" were the sentiments expressed by one and all.

The following day Charlie and I had to return to our respective coal-mining valleys, and after the excitement of the weekend, the prospect of another year ahead of us down the pit seemed an anticlimax. The send-off party at Troy station lingered in my mind and was kept alive by the sight of the recruitment posters that began to appear in the valley. Within a month, on 2 September 1914, I was walking into Caerphilly with five other lads from the Windsor colliery, intent on signing up.

Enlistment

– What happened when you signed up?

A RECRUITMENT OFFICE had been opened in Caerphilly and it was there that we accepted the king's shilling. We were divided between two different regiments, either the Welsh Regiment or the Prince Albert's Somerset Light Infantry. I was assigned to the latter, and thought the name sounded rather grand. We were not allowed to return home but were given a free train pass from Caerphilly to Cardiff where we were to report to an assembly point at a school. On the way to Caerphilly station I chanced to see Mr Harry Jenkins, the Windsor colliery under-manager, a massive man who had just been giving evidence at the police station. We gathered round him excitedly, told him that we had just enlisted, and asked him to inform our families and employers. He promised to do all this, said that he was proud of us and gave us each the considerable sum of ten shillings for wages due. He came with us to the station and waved us off, saying he'd see us all again before Christmas.

On arrival at Rhymney Station in Cardiff we were met by an uniformed sergeant who marched us to the school, together with many other lads who had been on the same train. There were scores of us in the school, all being mustered into our assigned regiments. There was a group of lads from Tonypandy who were insistent that they didn't want to be separated; they didn't care which regiment they were put into as long as they could all stay together. These Tonypandy Pals, as they became known, were also placed in the Somerset Light Infantry. Looking a motley band in our civilian clothes, we formed up under a regimental corporal and were marched to another part of the building where we were given tea and sandwiches. I remember the great variety of hats we wore: trilbies, boaters, caps and bowlers. We were issued with two blankets each and told to find somewhere on the floor to sleep. Luckily the weather was warm and we were a group of friends. Four blankets between two are much more useful than two blankets for one: we formed pairs, putting one blanket below us and one on top of us, leaving two to be rolled into a comfortable pillow. We were not allowed out of the school: there were sentries posted at the gates. Although we had all volunteered, it seemed as though we were prisoners.

Taunton, Aldershot and Woking

– Where did they send you next?

AT DAY BREAK the following morning, we awoke to a roar of sergeants. We were told to fold our blankets and place them in bundles of ten. After breakfast we were marched into Cardiff to board another train, this one bound for Taunton, beyond the Severn Tunnel. We were supervised on the journey by the sergeants and corporals, and on arrival in Taunton were marched to the regimental barracks. Here we were given a meal in the regimental dining room and then allocated to our various platoons and companies. My three mates and I joined the Tonypandy Pals in No. 12 Platoon of C Company. A sergeant and a corporal from the barracks were assigned to each platoon. Later we were introduced to the officers. Some of these were professional soldiers who had many years' service behind them. Indeed they were now too old for active service. (As it happened, I was too young. Back in Caerphilly I had given my age as eighteen in order to qualify for enlistment although my eighteenth birthday was still over six months away.) We were each issued with personal kit: soap, a razor, a shaving brush and a towel. We were also given a passbook with our personal number. Mine was 14126 Gordon, A.E., miner, Wales.

Three days later and another train journey, this time to Aldershot. Here the atmosphere was much stricter. All the officers and instructors were active soldiers who knew their trade. Their job was to train us and train us quickly and this they did with merciless efficiency. We each had an individual iron bedstead with our own bedding. Beds had to be made to a set standard ready for inspection. Likewise, our kit had to be presented for inspection to a given standard. There were parades and duties to perform: fatigue duties, potato peeling, cleaning the camp. The idea behind all this was to instil discipline into us – as if working underground hadn't done that already! But the food was good and the comradeship of this Welsh platoon as fine above as below ground.

Inspections, inspections, inspections, and then, just as we were getting used to the Aldershot routine, off we went again. The entire Seventh Battalion of the Somerset Light Infantry was route marched to the Inkerman Barracks, Woking. Here we were issued with Kitchener's Army uniforms, a blue serge suit and matching Glengarry hat, grey woollen shirts and underpants, together with new boots. The sizes were all a bit approximate and we exchanged items amongst ourselves until we had uniforms that fitted. One of the boys was a tailor and helped do alterations. We had orders to send our civilian clothes home.

Promotion

– You were promoted to corporal while at the Inkerman Barracks, weren't you?

YES, to my great surprise. One day the platoon officer asked me if I would like to attend a seven-day intensive course on orientation. I had enjoyed map and compass work at school in Llangattock and taken an interest in surveying down the pit so I was naturally excited at the prospect of learning more. There were twelve of us on the course, the purpose of which, as it turned out, was to select four company scouts and eight platoon scouts to be responsible for field manoeuvres. I was selected a company scout.

There followed extensive field manoeuvres in the surrounding countryside by day and night. Generally, these manoeuvres were conducted one company at a time, but one day it was announced that the whole battalion was going out at night on manoeuvres in the vicinity of the Devil's Punch Bowl. The old colonel sent for me and requested that I accompany him as scout at the head of the battalion. I was very proud. We set off from the barracks under cover of darkness, not returning until the early hours of the following morning.

The following morning we were allowed free time, assembling after lunch for an address by the colonel. He revealed that the night exercise had been observed by umpires, that everything had gone very well, and that we were all to be congratulated. As I was getting ready to go into town for my off-duty time, my platoon officer called for me. To my surprise, I was told I had been granted a week's leave.

I returned by train to Monmouth eager to show Mam my new uniform. Noah beamed with pride at the sight of it, whilst Mam busied herself with needle and thread taking in seams so that everything fitted perfectly. Noah advised me to grease my new boots. When I returned to the barracks, my pals rushed to tell me that my name had been posted up in orders and that I'd been promoted to the rank of corporal. Now, still two months before my eighteenth birthday, I was a corporal in the British army!

Sailing for France

— *When did you leave for France?*

FOLLOWING FURTHER TRAINING at Inkerman Barracks, we transferred to Rollestone Camp on Salisbury Plain where our training intensified. Here younger officers took over command: Colonel Troyte-Bullock, Major White and, for our "C" company, Captain Hatt, son of the Mayor of Bath. We were properly organised: sixteen men to a section, four sections to a platoon, four platoons to a company, four companies to a battalion. In charge of each section was a lance corporal, of each platoon a second lieutenant, of each company a captain, with the colonel in overall command of the battalion. There were so many different ranks: company sergeant majors, battalion sergeant majors, stores officers and stores sergeants, not to mention the cooks and members of the band. The officer in charge of our platoon was a young college graduate with the rank of second lieutenant. Below him was Sergeant Anstey, an older man who had been called up from the reserve and put back into active service. I was the corporal for number 12 platoon of "C" company.

In the middle of February 1915 we were all granted a week's leave but given to understand that we would be leaving for France upon our return. It was close to the end of March when we were given our marching orders. We were instructed to parcel up any private property, address it clearly and turn it in to the stores. The entire battalion formed up in the dark of night, section by section, with field kitchens and stores vans, the whole procession preceded by military band, drums beating and bugles blowing. We marched to Amesbury Station, where a train was awaiting us, carrying us on through the night to Salisbury and on to Dover. Walking the sea front in the early hours of the morning before embarking the ferry, I came across a statue to Charles Rolls of the Hendre, erected in 1912 to commemorate his round trip flight across the Channel, just a few months before his death in the disaster at Bournemouth. For the first time, I felt anxious about my own return, and the example of Charles Rolls helped steady my nerves.

Before embarking the ferry, we drew haversack rations and refilled our water bottles. This was my first experience of the sea. It was a rough crossing, but although some of my pals were sick I managed to avoid feeling ill. Mam had told me to head for the open deck and to look out to sea. She had learned to do that coming back from America and, as usual, hers was good advice. The journey took up the entire day and it was late at night when we arrived at St John's Camp, outside Boulogne. Within an hour or so of our arrival, the field kitchen was supplying us with hot soup and tea. We drew two blankets each from stores and settled into our bell tents for the night, eight men per tent. We had no trouble sleeping.

Through France

– How soon was it before you moved up to the front line?

WE WERE WAKENED at dawn and told to fold our blankets and stack them in tens next to the store vans. Breakfast was served at the field kitchen. By seven o'clock we were pulling out of Boulogne Station in open trucks pulled by the largest steam engine we had ever seen. Eventually, with much stopping and starting, we reached St. Omer. Here we formed up and marched out of the town, seeking shelter from the rain in a large wood. The field kitchens supplied the mid-day meal, each soldier parading with his billycan for stew and two slices of bread. We were then told to get as much rest as possible, that we would have more food at five o'clock, and that this meal would be followed by a long, hard march to the front line.

So it was. As we set off on the march we were told that we were now within range of long-range enemy gunfire. We were to consider ourselves in action and act accordingly. We marched, broke for rest, marched on, broke for rest and marched on again, halting at last just over the Belgian border at Watou Camp, outside the town of Poperinge.

The rain was making conditions under foot impossible; in places the mud was several feet deep. We were told it was even worse on the front line. Before turning in we had a supper of soup and biscuits. As we settled into our tents that night, I could see that some men's feet were raw from marching. We had not had a chance to change any clothing since Rollestone Camp. This was to be the last time the whole battalion was together as one body. From this time onwards, we split into companies, with each company moving on its own and with communication between companies maintained by runners.

Beyond Poperinge was the Ypres road. As we advanced along it we couldn't fail to notice that we were approaching the front line. The sound of firing grew louder, trees and vegetation were destroyed, and villages lay in ruins. The Very lights in the night sky revealed the front line was a horseshoe with the 7th Somerset Light Infantry advancing surely towards its centre. As we got closer we were instructed not to talk, not to smoke or strike a match and to proceed in single file. Each section was now spaced well apart. We trudged on in the shelter of the hedges and roadside bank, running ahead quickly when this cover was broken. Machine gun bullets were falling in the vicinity but they had travelled a long distance and were almost spent; you could tell this by the sound they made.

Flanders

– Did you meet any friends or family on the Western Front?

STOPS FOR REST AND REFRESHMENT were now taken quickly. Biscuit replaced bread in our rations and the water now had an unpleasant taste to it. During one such stop we met a unit returning from the front line. Like us they were marching Indian file, but unlike us they looked very much the worse for wear. They were tired and dirty and had many men wounded. To my astonishment, I recognised my fellow lodger, Jim Davies, filing past me, the billiard marker from the Institute in Abertridwr. I knew that, as a former guardsman, he'd been called up and it turned out that he'd been placed in the Shropshire Light Infantry. We, the Somersets, were relieving them. Jim told me that my uncle, Ted Kidley, was also in the vicinity. Like Jim, he was with the Shropshires. He was in "D" company which was further up the line, where a bridge crossed over the canal. They were waiting for us to relieve them. The canal, when we reached it, was in a dreadful condition, nearly empty and with dead mules floating in the water. We crossed the bridge to relieve "D" company who occupied a communication trench that led to the front line. Here I found my uncle lying on the floor of a dugout with a few of his mates eating corned beef from a can. He looked awful. "I never thought I'd see you here, Alf!" was about all he managed to say, although he did offer to share his corned beef with me. "How are you keeping?" I asked lamely. "Not so bad," he replied, staring through me all the while. "It's been worse."

A complete relief operation would sometimes take several days to execute depending on conditions. There was a network of trenches, starting with the third or reserve line, then a second line leading on to the front line. The relieving unit would occupy the reserve line while the displaced men moved forward to the second line, and the second to the front. The former front line troops would then drop back to the reserve line. Uncle Ted had seen all this before. We shook hands and parted, he to go back, me to go forward.

In the reserve line a soldier could take off his boots, but not his clothes, and was involved in a variety of service duties, such as fetching rations or trench repairs, for which the men in the front line

parties as little treats for his boys. "All right, sergeant," he would say. "They've done frightfully well. Let them fall out now and come with me to the canteen. I've arranged tea and cakes for all their good work!" No wonder he was popular!

Recreation and Romance

– Didn't you meet your future wife at Rollestone?

WHILE SERVING as an anti-gas instructor at Rollestone Camp my health improved sufficiently for me to revive my interest in sport. I took up running in the countryside around the camp and entered a number of cross-country competitions of varying lengths ranging from three to a marathon of twenty-six miles. Learning to pace oneself and developing both physical and mental stamina were important for all types of long-distance running. I trained with Sergeant Whiteman of the Notts and Derby Regiment and Sergeant Foyle of the Wiltshires. Our trainer was a delightful Indian mess sergeant who ran as swiftly and gracefully as one of the Hendre deer.

The competitions were organised by the English Southern Counties Cross-country Association from which organisation I received a first prize gold-centred medal, and a second prize silver medal at another event, which was won by Sergeant Whiteman. I recall a particularly gruelling seven-mile event at which I represented my unit in full marching order. There were all kinds of obstacles: fences, netting, barrels to crawl through, ropes to climb and a final up-hill run which finished after fording a stream. I was quite exhausted after this ordeal and excused duty for several days afterwards by the medical officer. I did win the first prize, however: a cellophane matchbox cover with the regimental crest printed on it presented to me by our beaming Officer. It was the honour of winning which counted the most, he observed.

Romance was in the air at Rollestone in the final twelve months of the war. The demonstration dugout we had constructed for anti-gas training was in great demand by courting couples and it fell to me to try to put a stop to this unauthorised use of facilities. To deter nocturnal visitors we rigged up a trip wire that would tip a tin of lime wash over any culprit. The following morning the mess was buzzing with gleeful tidings. One of the officers was furious because someone had tipped lime wash over his best suit the previous night. It was difficult for me to keep a straight face. More subtly, one of the specialist officers would tell me on a daily basis that he needed to go into Salisbury to replenish the supply of safety pins used for fitting the gas masks. We must have had thousands of safety pins from all those trips to town, but he was a delightful man, a commercial traveller from Bristol before the war, and we let him be. We were all yearning for affection to soothe the horrors of war.

It was at Rollestone that I met my future wife, Dorothy Beales. Doll, as she was known, was serving as a cook with the WAAC. She was from North Shields in Northumberland and had the most beautiful long tresses of auburn hair. Her father and brothers were all merchant seamen. We married in her home town on 26 December 1918. Doll obtained extended Christmas leave on compassionate grounds and my eldest brother Jack, another survivor of the war, was our best man. We were to name our first-born child, Catherine Rollestone: Catherine after my mother-in-law and Rollestone after the place where her parents first met.

Back down the pit

– What happened to you when the war was over?

WHEN THE ARMISTICE was signed on the eleventh hour of the eleventh day of the eleventh month 1918, I was released for mining work under class "W". I parted from Doll, who remained at Rollestone, and set off for Abertridwr, calling briefly at Well Cottage in Newcastle to see my parents on the way. The Windsor Colliery in Abertridwr, like so many other pits, had been short of labour during the war and many of the workings had been closed. These workings had filled with water and were generally in an unsafe condition. The management wanted us to start quickly on what was to be the long and unpleasant task of de-watering, rendering safe and reopening these neglected workings.

Although we were four years older, those of us who returned could hardly claim to be experienced miners: digging trenches was not the same as digging coal. Nevertheless, the shortage of labour and the urgency of the work meant that I found myself employed as a skilled collier with my own stall to work and with a boy as an assistant. We started work on the de-watering, using buckets to fill two water tubs on a tram which, when full, were carried away by a haulier. We were paid one shilling per tub of water, filling about eight tubs per shift. There were about twenty of us doing this job and it took months to get the water out of the workings. We joked about how similar this work was to that in the trenches in Flanders, but at least here we had some pay, a clean bed and above all the comradeship of work-mates and the love of family. Very soon I would have a wife and home of my own.

After our wedding in North Shields on Boxing Day, Doll and I journeyed to Wales, first paying a visit to my parents in Newcastle, then moving to Abertridwr to set up home. I remembered Mam telling me when I was little how the birds built their nests bit by bit and Doll and I took pleasure in doing the same. My wife had no experience of a mining community but had just the right sociable disposition for the Welsh Valleys. She was a wonderful cook, housewife and, with the arrival of Kit on 8 July 1919, mother.

Homes of our own

— Where did you live after you were married?

OUR FIRST HOME was in High Street where we rented two rooms. There were no pithead baths in those days so Doll would have a bath tub ready for me at the end of the shift. She even rolled some cigarettes ready for me. I would arrive home soaking wet and filthy dirty. My work clothes were dried on the fire guard and in the mornings they would be so stiff that I would have to go into the back yard and beat them against the wall to make them flexible enough to put back on. I was on a day shift that started at six so I was up at four thirty in the morning.

Returning to the pit was disastrous for my health. I had been on the mend at Rollestone but back underground my strength disappeared and I had to go to the manager and ask for a lighter job. It may have been the lingering effect of the gas; perhaps my arm had needed more time to recuperate. Whatever the cause it gave us great anxiety. A lighter job meant less money, and we now had difficulty making ends meet. We moved out of the apartments in High Street and moved in temporarily with my uncle and aunt, Rose and Joe Green at 27, Graig-y-Fedw. They couldn't have been more hospitable.

My new job was as an assistant to a repairer underground named

John Lloyd. John was also a baker who delivered his bread by horse and cart in the village in the mornings so it suited him to work the afternoon shift. With John Lloyd and his team the language underground was Welsh and to begin with I was lost in the conversations, recognising only the few words with which my stepfather Noah Vaughan had peppered his English, but gradually I learned and grew in confidence. John Lloyd was a member of Beulah Baptist Chapel in Thomas Street and very pleased to hear that my stepfather was of the same persuasion. One day the minister, the Revd. J. J. Morgan, called at our home in the hope that we would come to services but somehow I couldn't bring myself to go. Something had snapped inside me on the Somme.

While working for John Lloyd I made friends with an elderly pumpsman from the Forest of Dean, John Dudfield. He invited Doll and I to move in with him and his wife at 17, Graig-y-Fedw and that we did, not wanting to impose on my uncle and aunt for any longer than was necessary. Mrs Dudfield was as deaf as she was house proud. She would not light a fire in the grate in the mornings for fear the dust would spoil the brasses on the mantle shelf; she scrubbed the floor, then put down matting to keep the floor clean, then put newspaper on the mats to keep them clean also. Doll was expected to approach housework in the same way and this got her down. Between us we were getting to the end of our tether and we returned to my Aunt Rose, just a few doors away. She had seen how things were developing. Soon afterwards, however, Mrs Dudfield passed away and old John decided to return to the Forest of Dean, offering us the tenancy of his house. This was a lucky break indeed! It was a good solid stone-built six-room house where we continued to live until I left the valley in 1938. At one point we were offered the house for sale at £300, a sum we couldn't contemplate. In those days we couldn't raise three hundred shillings, much less three hundred pounds!

Strikes

– Weren't labour conditions bad in the coalfield at this time?

JUST AS DOLL AND I were beginning to see some sort of future take shape, the three month strike of 1921 knocked us back to rock bottom again. Doll went to stay with her parents in North Shields while I ventured back to the Hendre to work on the drives on the estate. The estate manager did not like miners and tried to give me a lesson in the perils of trades unionism but he knew I was local and directed me to the drive foreman who, by good fortune, turned out to be my Uncle John Kidley. He was the son of my maternal grandfather, now dead, and had taken over his father's duties on the estate and lived in the cottage on the estate where I was born, The Garrow. I worked on the drives under Uncle John Kidley for six weeks for two pounds seven shillings a week. I lodged with my mother in Well Cottage, sending the balance of my earnings to my wife. Somehow we managed to stay out of debt.

The strike over, we returned to Abertridwr and I went back to work underground. On 30 April 1922, our second child was born, Doreen Constance. These were difficult times across the coalfield and tension mounted rapidly after the owners cut our wages in 1925. The month of May 1926 came as another blow just as we were again getting back on our feet. In the glorious spring of that year the dispute between the miners and the pit owners reached such a pitch that the General Council of the TUC called a General Strike throughout the country in support of the miners. It lasted for nine days. The pits were closed, and there was no transport in the valley. Although the General Strike was called off, the miners continued in dispute for six long months. The prospect of mounting debt as we paid out on food and lodging was alarming. The only ones to benefit were the pit ponies who were brought to the surface to enjoy the sunshine. But for all of us, anxieties mounted with the onset of winter. I was fortunate in securing some temporary work as a hod carrier on a building site opposite my home, my experience at Hilston Manor proving useful. Doll took in four lodgers from the building site. She toiled away cheerfully at her housework, cooking and washing for her husband and four lodgers, with our three young daughters to look after too until, at the end of November, we miners returned underground, defeated.

Mine rescue

— You were very active in mine rescue with the St John's Ambulance, weren't you?

I'VE ALREADY MENTIONED the combined effects that Senghennydd and the Somme had on me. I had dedicated myself to saving life, not to destroying it. And, if I'd had the courage to speak my mind when the Revd. J.J. Morgan had suggested that I go to his chapel, I should have told him that I preferred to see lives saved in this life, not the next. Once we were settled in our own place in Graig-y-Fedw, I devoted almost all my spare time to mine rescue work, taking county education committee evening classes in Caerphilly and involving myself in the work of the St John's Ambulance. Underground, St John's Ambulance volunteers "carried the box", that is, we were looked to for first aid whenever there was an accident, which was far too often. One local nickname for the mine owners, Powell Dyffryn, was "Poverty and Death", suggested by the initials painted on the coal trucks that trundled along the Aber line that ran at the foot of our garden.

On 29 February 1924, a leap year, our third child Stella was born. Also in that year the local St John's Ambulance group was officially constituted as the Windsor Corps of the St John's Ambulance Priory of Wales. Two years later, on 26 April 1926, I became Superintendent and Captain of Rescue Work. On two evenings a week we organised large classes for men and women, boys and girls. By 1929, we had raised sufficient funds in the valley to start work on building of our own St. John's Ambulance Hall in Williams Street. This facility was officially opened in 1938. As captain of the Windsor colliery first aid team, I took part in numerous competitions held in the valleys in those days. These competitions created interest and enthusiasm for mine safety. Seven times we won the gold medal in the Rhymney valley championships.

With my growing expertise on mine safety, I found the high accident rate in the coalfield unacceptable and when, in 1936, a new position of Colliery Safety Officer was proposed for the Windsor colliery, I successfully applied for the job. I couldn't have dreamed of a job I more wanted to do. I had scope to go anywhere in the mine, day or night, as duty called. One early innovation I was responsible for was a system of personal record cards detailing the sickness and accident history of every man underground. I was also keen to see the introduction of more protective equipment, such as safety guards on certain machines, safer working practices, stages for men to work on in high places and improved roof supports. It was not a job to make you popular with either men or the officials – both sides resisted change for their own reasons – but I could tell from my records that the changes were for the better. There were fewer accidents and lives were being saved.

Area Safety Engineer

– Why did you move from Abertridwr?

SOME TIME IN 1938 the colliery General Manager, Mr. Douglas Hann, sent for me. I had no knowledge of what was afoot. Mr. Hann and his assistant Mr. David Griffiths reviewed my safety campaign in the colliery at length, complimented me on what had been achieved, then offered me the position of Area Safety Engineer for the Rhymney district of Powell Dyffryn, giving me responsibility for underground safety in eighteen pits. They wanted the systems I had put in place at the Windsor colliery to be applied throughout the district. This was a challenge I was delighted to accept.

My office was to be at the Britannia Colliery near Pengam, some fifteen miles distant up the Rhymney valley. For each of the larger pits for which I was responsible, we appointed colliery safety officers; smaller pits shared a safety officer. Our two eldest daughters had now left the nest. Kit was in Fairford, Gloucestershire, working as a nanny; Doreen was in service at Waystone Leys, outside Monmouth. Doll, Stella and I left 17, Graig-y-Fedw, our home for close on twenty years, for a company house near the colliery at Britannia Terrace.

It's amazing how quickly an apparently straightforward job description can turn into something completely different. The outbreak of war added a raft of new responsibilities to my job, including fire fighting and first aid in civil defence. We had to draw up plans to protect the mines from air raids. All the usual mining hazards continued, of course, and I put on a series of demonstrations of safety procedures to officials and workmen at our surface centre at Britannia colliery. Often, I would prefer to demonstrate on the job. Once convinced, the men would be my greatest supporters in the drive for better safety in the mines.

Although lacking in paper qualifications, I had been appointed because of my practical experience and proven track record. Nevertheless, it was clear that having the necessary paper qualifications would give me more authority in the eyes of the higher officials. I therefore studied by correspondence with the Universal Mining College in Cardiff, successfully passing first the Under Manager's Certificate, then, at the second attempt, the Colliery Manager's Certificate. The latter, passed first class, was dated 23 April 1945, my forty-eighth birthday. The sense of achievement was wonderful.

The winter of 1947

– The year 1947 was a memorable one, wasn't it?

THE WINTER OF 1947 was particularly severe with heavy drifting snow. Our new home was 1,400 feet up the mountain on the Monmouthshire side of the Rhymney valley. The drifting snow reached the second floor windows of the house and I would walk to the colliery along the top of the hawthorn hedge taking care not to fall through, as happened to some. Sometimes I had to walk over the mountain through the drifts to a neighbouring colliery because I had no more petrol coupons. On another occasion a group of us helped dig out a stranded passenger train that was stuck in the drifts for seventeen hours.

But they say every cloud has a silver lining, and so it was in 1947. On New Year's Day 1947, Welsh miners celebrated the end of private ownership of the mines and the birth of the National Coal Board. Few tears were shed for the private owners; as far as pit safety was concerned the way ahead now seemed altogether brighter.

One unexpected problem that arose after the war was the impact of food rationing and the realisation that a decline in output at the mine had coincided with the introduction of food rationing. Although nothing was said openly, I suspected that many miners were simply short of food. Discreet enquiries were made in the various pits and a pattern soon emerged of fatigue caused by under-nourishment. Nothing could be more inimical to mine safety. Men were going short of protein, eating sandwiches filled with beetroot instead of cheese, so that their families didn't go short. As a result of a major campaign we were able to secure a larger ration of cheese for miners and, eventually, the introduction of colliery canteens.

In 1950 the National Eisteddfod came to Caerphilly and my Britannia team were placed first in the shot firing competition, *tanio dan ddaear*. In 1952 I took charge of airborne dust control. Since Senghennydd we knew all about the danger of dust causing underground fires but the prevalence of pneumoconiosis was now also causing concern. A survey of the Rhondda Fach revealed that half the miners there had the disease. We organised a march through Cardiff later that year to draw the public's attention to this modern Black Death. Back down the pit, I introduced a series of wet techniques to reduce airborne dust: wet cutting, wet boring, roadway consolidation and so on. Mining remained a dangerous occupation and there were pit explosions in the years following nationalisation at Bedwas and New Nantgarw. The Bedwas explosion occurred on 10 October 1952 at 6:30 pm. One man was killed and nineteen injured, several with severe burns that needed special treatment in the hospital at Chepstow. But we had everyone out of the mine by 8:30 pm. At Nantgarw an explosion occurred on 9 May 1955 at 5:40 pm. This time we succeeded in evacuating the pit in less than two hours with only four men injured with slight burns. There was a second explosion on the following day in which two men were killed. The official inquiry revealed breaches in underground safety procedures. When I left the coalfield the following month our area safety office at Britannia Colliery had established an international reputation for mine safety and delegations visited us from all over Europe.

By car from Wales

– How did you come to leave south Wales?

WE MOVED FROM PENGAM in September 1955, Doll and I in our Austin 60 ahead of the removal van. I had been offered a promotion I couldn't refuse as an Area Safety and Health Engineer in the Cannock Chase area of the Staffordshire coalfield in the English Midlands. It would be a rupture to leave all our old friends but Doll and I wanted to save enough money to buy our own house for my retirement and with this new job I would at last be able to earn enough for us to realise this dream. We moved into a pleasant National Coal Board house on the Hednesford Road in Rugeley, called "Woodthorne", with a fine kitchen garden. The house overlooked the Derbyshire peaks and fresh milk could be obtained from Mr Woodcock's farm opposite.

Leaving Wales by car I thought back over the changes my life had seen. A childhood spent entirely on foot with an occasional ride on a pony. Then, going down the pit, again on foot in the company of pit ponies. I had seen the new-fangled motor cars at the Hendre when they were merely rich man's toys. Then, when working at Britannia colliery, I had bought my first car, an Austin Seven, to get around the various pits in my district. There was no driving licence in those days, and our first venture out of the Aber valley ended in near disaster in Caerphilly, as we narrowly avoided a shop window after failing to turn the corner at Piccadilly. We had to get out and push when our little car became stuck on Caerphilly mountain, but it did once oblige us with a trip to the Gower, with a suitcase on the roof and deckchairs tied to the spare wheel on the back.

Our Austin 60 pulled up in front of our new house in Rugeley and, as our furniture was carried in, we inspected the garden. Doll spotted a neighbour and went over to introduce herself. "I hear you're from Wales," she was brusquely informed. "I want you to know that we're not in and out of each other's houses here. We keep ourselves to ourselves." We had arrived in a foreign country and a whole new set of challenges awaited us!

For a full list of our publications
both in English and Welsh, ask for
your free copy of our
full-colour, 40-page Catalogue.
Alternatively, just surf into our
website at:
www.ylolfa.com

Talybont Ceredigion Cymru/Wales SY24 5AP
ffôn 0044 (0)1970 832 304 *ffacs* 832 782 *isdn* 832 813
e-bost ylolfa@ylolfa.com *y we* www.ylolfa.com

Other publications

Aberdyfi: The Past Recalled – Hugh M. Lewis £6.95
You Don't Speak Welsh! – Sandi Thomas £5.95
Ar Bwys y Ffald – Gwilym Jenkins £7.95
Blodeuwedd – Ogmore Batt £5.95
Choose Life – Phyllis Oostermeijer £5.95

Order your books online at
www.ylolfa.com

For more information about the Dinas imprint contact Lefi Gruffudd,
General Editor at Y Lolfa

Y Lolfa Cyf., Talybont, Ceredigion SY24 5AP
e-mail ylolfa@ylolfa.com
website www.ylolfa.com
tel. (01970) 832 304
fax 832 782
isdn 832 813